D1592139

Historic Cottages
of Mackinac Island

Historic Cottages of Mackinac Island

Text By
Susan Stites &
Lea Ann Sterling

Photography By
Lanny Sterling &
Lea Ann Sterling

opposite: David Hogg's West Bluff
Cottage White Pines, p. 52

Text © 2001 by Susan Stites
and Lea Ann Sterling

Photographs © 2001 by Lanny
and Lea Ann Sterling unless
otherwise credited

Ornamental lettering © 2001
by Elizabeth Miniotis

Book Design by Elizabeth Miniotis

Published by Arbutus Press
P. O. Box 234
Mayfield, Michigan 49666
Arbutuspress@traverse.com

LCCN 2001086451
ISBN 0-9665316-1-2
ISBN 0-9665316-2-0 Limited Edition
10 9 8 7 6 5 4 3 2 1

First Edition
Printed in Singapore by Imago

right: credit Mackinac State Historic Parks, Michigan

To
Amelie and Daniel, Mariah and Libby
Bob and Heather, Hunter, Mackenzie,
Rick and Stacey, Sydney,
Chrissy and Craig, Griffin and Greta Rose
and To Ted

The Authors would like to thank The Mackinac Island cottagers and residents, especially Candi Dunnigan, Charlotte Schmitt, Sharon Hahn, Shannon Schueller, Rosalie Roush, Cordie Puttkammer, Richard Wilson, Fritz Bennett, Charlotte Ernster, Robert Raisch, Audrey Gallery, Lois Rohder, Marvin Dziabis, John Gilpin, Penny Barr, Bill Porter, Linda Kughn, Alice Myron, Dan and Amelia Musser, Carol Rearick, Jeannette Doud, Lois Findley, Tom Tellefson, Trish Martin, Fred Holt, Aileen Poole Koehler, Bill Early, Jim Bogan, Jane Manikoff, Lin Sheppard, LeAndra Langdon, Kristin Lewand, Elizabeth Murcko, Jim Lenfesty, Lynn Williams, Kitty Hannabass, Michelle and Randy Stuck, Dennis Dufina, Marianne Miller, Robert Benjamin, Ann Bronfman, Clayton and Anna Timmons, Robert Benser, and Michael and Jane Bacon.

Also, Barb Siepker, Michael Matts, Monte Reed, M. L. Silverthorne, Jody Wardle, Jim Pauling, Chris Matyn, Village Press, Diane Frankovich, Lou DeFalco, Steve Brisson, and Nancy Gram.

And, the staff of The Newberry Library; Bentley Historical Library; Clarke Historical Library; Burton Historical Collections; State of Michigan Library; Chicago Historical Society Research Center; Indiana Historical Society; Indiana State Library; Peoria Public Library; Bowling Green State University Center for Archival Collections; W.G. Rhea Library—W.O. Inman Genealogy Room of Paris, Tennessee; St. Joseph Historical Society; Mackinac Island Public Library; St. Ignace Public Library; Edmonds Historical Society; Grand Rapids Public Library; St. Louis Genealogical Society; Northwestern Michigan College; Traverse Area District Library; Traverse City Print & Copy Center; Village Press; and Allen County, Indiana Public Library.

A special thanks to Phil Porter, Kathryn Eckert, Judi Bagaloff, Lorna Straus, Brian Dunnigan.

right: Ezra Barnard's East Bluff Cottage Montezuma, p.21

CONTENTS

Dear Reader,

Mackinac Island is one of America's greatest treasures of beauty and history. The Island's historic summer cottages make it even more of a treasure. I was blessed to live and raise my family in two of these cottages. After twelve years in the Michigan Governor's Summer Residence, and wanting to remain on the Island, Soapy and I bought The Pines on the West Bluff. I am very impressed to learn the history of these treasures captured in *Historic Cottages of Mackinac Island.*

Former Governor Williams would have heartily supported this project. He felt strongly that the historic buildings on Mackinac Island should be preserved. He made the restoration of Fort Mackinac, then becoming a pile of rubble, a Michigan priority. He knew that we learn much about our history through our buildings.

This book is striking proof that our history can be learned through our historic buildings. Authors Susan Stites and Lea Ann Sterling tell an important part of the history of Mackinac Island through each summer cottage. Lanny and Lea Ann Sterling's photographs capture the beauty of these treasures. Through their work, Stites and the Sterlings invite us all to know and protect these treasures, to keep them unspoiled for the future.

Nancy Williams Gram
Former First Lady of Michigan

February 11, 2001

Governor and Mrs. G. Mennen Williams, Gery, Nancy, Wendy, and "Torchy" on Mackinac Island
credit Nancy Williams Gram

INTRODUCTION

From 1883 through 1902, the *Daily Resorter* newspaper, published in Petoskey, Michigan, provided the hype and gossip to keep tourists and summer residents apprised of the comings and goings on Mackinac Island. Published during the resort season, June through September, the *Daily Resorter* provides a portal to an important aspect of America's industrial era: industrialists at play. The adults blended social and business activity on Mackinac Island while the children of these politicians and businessmen roamed the cedar woods as playmates, some to marry years later. The families marked their place in Island history by building rambling multi-storied cottages and by cutting business deals here. They acquired prosperity by compounding it with opportunity, producing the ultimate occupation, "a capitalist." These were the original cottage owners of Mackinac Island.

As early as 1850, some came and stayed at The Mackinaw or St. Cloud Hotels for a few weeks or even a month but found them inadequate for spending the season. Inquiries from influential people drifted in to Fort Mackinac officials, requesting non-military use of the grounds near the idled Fort, particularly on the prominent bluffs. In 1849, such an inquiry came from Chicago pioneer and first mayor W.B. Ogden, who wrote to Major Charles Larnard, Commanding Officer at Fort Mackinac:

Dear Sir,

Residing as I do in the City of Chicago, I am desirous of securing a comfortable arrangement for spending the better portion of the summer months at Mackinac. The accommodations at Mackinac for receiving visitors are so meager that families are frequently unable on their arrival to obtain quarters at

above: The Silverthorne's enjoy a carriage ride, credit Jody Wardle collection

all convenient or comfortable.

The Government as you are aware retain as a military reservation the larger portion of the Island. And include in such reserve the entire bluff on the front and east side of it comprising all the most desirable situations for building upon in that vicinity. I beg leave therefore, through you and with your approbation, to make application to the Quarter Master General for permission to erect a summer lodge upon the Bluff East of the Garrison. This point is elected because of its easy access - its airy and sightly position - its convenience to the Hotel under the bluff, to which it can be readily connected by a flight of stairs - and because of its not appearing to be wanted for any purpose in connection with a post at the Military station…

Not until after Mackinac Island was proclaimed a National Park in 1875, did the Federal purse strings loosen and the U.S. War Department appropriate funds to survey, lease, and maintain building sites on the park's east and west bluffs. But another Chicago pioneer, Gurdon S. Hubbard, had secured a toe hold for selling lots from his eighty-acre parcel originally purchased in 1855. It was called Hubbard's Annex to the National Park, and the lots began turning into warranty deeds beginning in 1883 when the first nine lots sold. These sales restored Hubbard's bank account, which bottomed out after the 1871 Chicago Fire, and supplied the Midwest capitalists' demands for summer places on the Island.

Phebe Gehr, of Chicago, secured a lease on the East Bluff of the National Park to build the first cottage in 1885. Next to her, Charlotte Warren, of Chicago, built the second cottage within weeks. Suddenly, the cottagers were coming. They came from Davenport and Ft. Wayne, Chicago and Grand Rapids, Kalamazoo and Detroit, and even New Orleans and St. Joseph, Missouri. From Gehr's 1885 Carpenter Gothic cottage to V. W. Mather's small 1900 Colonial Revival, thirty-six cottages sprouted on the bluffs overlooking the village of Mackinac Island. Finally, Queen Anne, Shingle Style, and Gothic Revival cottages neighbored Carpenter Gothic, Classical Revival, and Colonial Revival. The cottagers not only built summer retreats, but built businesses, too.

The Michigan Central Railroad, Grand Rapids & Indiana Railroad, and Detroit & Cleveland Steamship Company owners erected cottages on either side of The Grand Hotel, not only for summer retreats but to keep an eye on their new business. They had formed The Mackinac Hotel Company in 1887 to build a grand hotel as a destination for their railroad and steamship passengers. The hotel they built set a high tone for Island social life, attracting the Midwest counterpart of Newport's eastern elite.

The Grand Hotel's style and opulence influenced new construction all over the Island. Some cottages only a year or two old, such as the West Bluff cottage owned by A. D. Hannah and another cottage owned by David Hogg, were completely torn down, redesigned, and rebuilt to emulate this new grand emblem of affluence.

Charles Caskey, builder of the Grand Hotel, and local builders Patrick Doud, A. G. Couchois, Frank Rounds, and A. W. Buckley worked at numerous construction projects. Workers were in short supply so some new leaseholders brought builders from their hometowns. Some recruited prestigious architects, such as Chicago's Frederick Perkins, who designed the Young Cottage, now, the Michigan Governor's Summer Residence. Perkins also designed the largest summer residence on the Island, Stonecliffe, for Michael Cudahy.

Historic Cottages of Mackinac Island explores the original cottage owners' biographies and peeks into the lives of some interesting subsequent owners. The cottage names derive from the early years, but many have changed with changing ownership. Wherever possible, the original or first known cottage name identifies it since Mackinac Island does not use street addresses and uses sign posts sparingly.

Stroll, trot, or spin along and marvel at the architecture and histories of these dwellings, but do not trespass. The East Bluff, West Bluff, and a few Lakeshore cottages are built on Michigan State Park land. The Annex and most cottages along the lakeshore are private property. ALL cottages are privately owned. Please respect them. Follow the route as mapped in *Historic Cottages of Mackinac Island*, or take the armchair tour. Discover the "imposing domiciles" created by opportunity, hard work, and the amazing success of their original owners.

May they "impose" and endure on this Island forever.

above: Mackinac Islanders at Sugar Loaf, credit Mackinac State Historic Parks, Michigan

The Cottages

1. Crow's Nest
2. Restmore
3. The Cliffs
4. Fisher Cottage
5. Ingleneuk
6. Montezuma
7. Yononte
8. Buena Vista
9. Far View
10. Tootle Cottage
11. Dolce Domum
12. Warren Cottage
13. Owen Cottage
14. Hamilton Cottage
15. Bursley Cottage
16. Craig Mawr
17. Morrison Cottage
18. Rest View
19. Bond Cottage
20. Sunrise Cottage

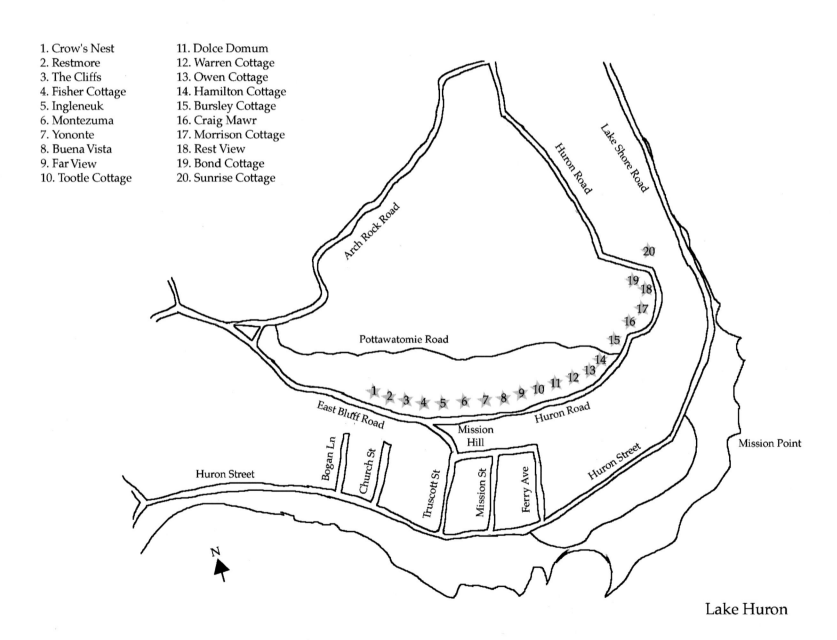

Mackinac Island
East Bluff
Cottages

Lake Shore Road

Huron Road

Arch Rock Road

Pottawatomie Road

East Bluff Road

Huron Road

Mission Hill

Bogan Ln

Church St

Truscott St

Mission St

Ferry Ave

Huron Street

Huron Street

Mission Point

N

Lake Huron

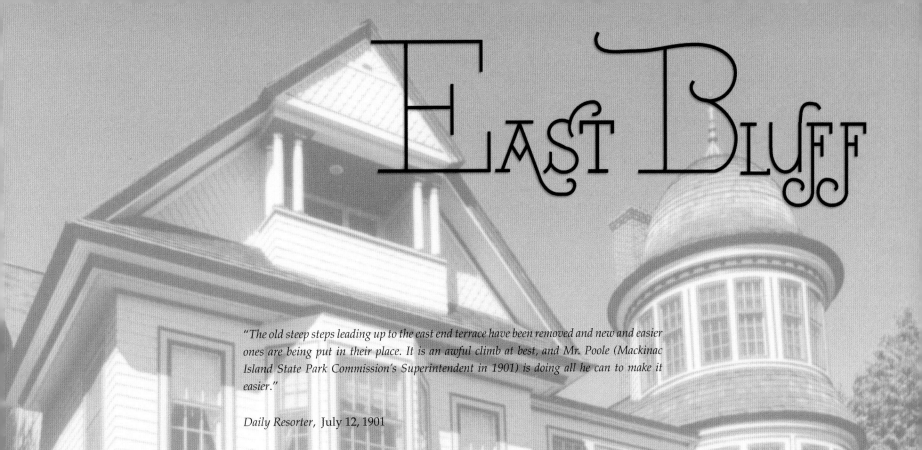

EAST BLUFF

"The old steep steps leading up to the east end terrace have been removed and new and easier ones are being put in their place. It is an awful climb at best, and Mr. Poole (Mackinac Island State Park Commission's Superintendent in 1901) is doing all he can to make it easier."

Daily Resorter, July 12, 1901

     In 1885, the East End witnessed the first private cottages built on government land on Mackinac Island. Charles Caskey, builder of The Grand Hotel, constructed Carpenter Gothic dwellings for Chicago's Phebe Gehr and her neighbor Charlotte Warren. Other cottages emerged in the next fifteen years when finally, East Bluff displayed twenty cottages in all. All have survived for over 100 years. Architectural style runs the gamut of individual taste with the Tootle Cottage being the only Neo Classical on the island.

1

VALCON ☙ OLIVE MATHER   1900
CROW'S NEST

In 1900, Dr. Valcoln Warsaw Mather with his wife, Olive S. (Keith) Mather, and their two children, Lelia and Henry, left the heat of Kansas City, Missouri, and came to spend the summer on Mackinac Island. Mather's medical career began in Kansas City, under the tutelage of Dr. V. R. Moss, and later, Dr. Joseph Feld. Mather completed his training at Pulte Medical College in Cincinnati, Ohio in 1873, and practiced briefly in West Virginia before returning home and establishing a practice in homeopathic medicine. He was a charter member of The Kansas City Homeopathic Medical College. The Mathers' son Henry joined his father's medical practice and became a surgeon of some note. Both Henry and his sister Lelia were young adults when their parents built the Mackinac Island cottage, and enjoyed exploring the nearby trails and footpaths.

Off into the cedar woods, west of the cottage, a trail leads to Anne's Tablet. This memorial honors Constance Fennimore Woolson, author of *Anne*, a popular 1880s novel about a young girl's adventures on Mackinac Island during the fur trade era. In admiration of their Aunt Constance, the Samuel Mather family from Cleveland erected Anne's Tablet in 1916. Samuel Mather and Valcoln W. Mather shared a common ancestor, Timothy Mather. Timothy's brother was Reverend Cotton Mather, known in history for his participation in the Salem Witch Trials.

Crow's Nest was the last cottage built on East Bluff. Local carpenter Frank Rounds constructed this small Colonial Revival cottage so that nothing obscured the view from the enclosed front porch. At the same time, its six-pane glass windows and the sidelights flanking the front door and the transom above, shelter the residents from the breezes off the Straits of Mackinac.

Crow's Nest stood unoccupied and in need of maintenance in the 1940s due to economic hard times. Like many boarded up cottages during these years, it reverted to the state. Attempting to find a buyer, the state asked $2,000 for the property. But even that meager amount fell short of finding buyers until Islanders Alan and Alice Sawyer offered $1,000 for the cottage on terms of $250 down and $100 per year.

"Mrs. Mather accompanied by her daughter, of Kansas City, is expected to arrive on the Northland next week to spend the season with her son, Dr. H. F. Mather, in the East End."

Daily Resorter, July 10, 1901

"Miss Bessie Stuart of Davenport Iowa is at "Restmore" cottage the guest of Miss Agnes Petersen also of Davenport. These two popular young ladies are having a very pleasant time in island social events in which they figure brilliantly."

Daily Resorter, July 31, 1901

HENRY & CLARA PETERSEN 1899
RESTMORE 2

This Colonial Revival is clad with clapboards on the first story and imbricate shingles on the second. The dominating gambrel roof teams up side by side with a tower for an enjoyable vista. A fascinating but obscure detail of Restmore is the small centrally located slot window crowned with a round arch hood in the peak of the gambrel dormer.

The cottage was built in 1899 for Henry F. Petersen and his wife Clara M. (King) Petersen of Davenport, Iowa. The family included three grown children, Arno Petersen, Mrs. W. F. Speers, and Mrs. George Decker, who all made the trek from Iowa to spend time at their Mackinac Island summer residence.

The Petersen family made their living in the merchandise business, supplying customers headed west toward the expanding frontier. Henry's father, J. H. Petersen, started the business in a log cabin with a storefront. In a few years, J.H.C. Petersen & Sons stockpiled enough market-able merchandise to fill a four-story department store in downtown Davenport. The acquisition of merchandise for Petersen's wholesale and retail business required Henry to travel extensively. On one trip from New York to California, a landslide near the "Culebra Cut" detained Petersen's ship at the Panama Canal. Food

deteriorated without refrigeration or ice on board, causing unsanitary conditions over the month-long trip, contributing to his illness and death in 1915. Five years later, the family sold their cottage to Leland Wood.

Leland was the son of Judge Edwin O. and Emily (Crocker) Wood of Flint, Michigan. Judge Edwin O. Wood expressed his love for Mackinac Island by writing the definitive two-volume reference book, *Historic Mackinac*, published in 1918. Another family contribution to the Island is a shelter covering the outlet of a natural spring, named Dwightwood Springs. It is a tribute to their son Dwight Hulbert Wood who died in 1905 while trying to save his brother's life. Judge Wood and his wife died a year apart, in 1918 and 1919.

HENRY FREEMAN
THE 3 CLIFFS
1890 – 1891

Simple ornamentation makes this gabled cottage elegant and unified, typical of Carpenter Gothic. The intersecting gable gives a symmetrical look to The Cliffs. The second floor window and balustraded balcony line up over the extra wide central stairway that rises to the ample first floor porch. Local contractor Mathias Elliot established himself as an important influence on East Bluff architecture. He built this cottage in 1890 and at least four others on East Bluff: Buena Vista and Restview in 1891, and Far View and Sunrise in 1892. His cottage styles varied, but his fee remained approximately $1500.

The first owner, Mr. Henry Freeman, worked as a cashier at the First National Bank in Ft. Wayne, Indiana. Active in social circles, he established a literary club named Qui Vive Club in 1878. He also associated in business with other East Bluff cottagers from Ft. Wayne, Indiana: Hamilton, Bursley, Taylor, and Bond.

In 1898, Mr. Freeman sold the cottage to Louisa Waldron of Elgin, Illinois.

In 1941, the Congregational Church, or the Little Stone Church as it is known on the Island, acquired the cottage. Twenty years later, the Fitzgerald family bought The Cliffs. The Fitzgerald name is notable through a prominent family member, two-term Governor of Michigan, Frank D. Fitzgerald. Governor Fitzgerald served his first term from 1935 to 1936. His second term, starting in January 1939, was cut short by his death in March of that year.

right: credit Mackinac State Historic Parks, Michigan

4 FISHER COTTAGE

ELSTNER and SARAH FISHER   1893

Carpenter G. W. Catell built a Dutch Colonial on this lot in 1893, but extensive renovation leaves little of the original structure. However, it still represents the historic architecture of the Island through its prominent three-stage corner tower topped with a bell roof.

The original owner, Elstner Fisher, from Cincinnati, Ohio, was forty years old when he had this cottage built. His career in the United States Navy and his job with railroad companies made him a traveling man. In the Navy, he was assigned duty on the steamer *Vandalia* and sailed in the

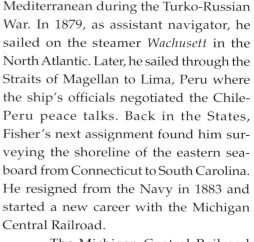

Mediterranean during the Turko-Russian War. In 1879, as assistant navigator, he sailed on the steamer *Wachusett* in the North Atlantic. Later, he sailed through the Straits of Magellan to Lima, Peru where the ship's officials negotiated the Chile-Peru peace talks. Back in the States, Fisher's next assignment found him surveying the shoreline of the eastern seaboard from Connecticut to South Carolina. He resigned from the Navy in 1883 and started a new career with the Michigan Central Railroad.

The Michigan Central Railroad kept him moving with its changing districts and divisions. As a trainmaster, Mr. Fisher's job required keeping the trains on schedule, as published in the timetables. He moved from Jackson, Michigan to Detroit where he helped the city survey for a tunnel under the Detroit River. His promotion to assistant superintendent took him to Hamilton, Ontario to become general superintendent and chief engineer of the Toronto, Hamilton & Buffalo railroad line.

Fisher apparently stayed in one place long enough to meet and marry Sarah Burt of Detroit. They had one child, a son, Philip (see East Bluff cottages 9 and 10).

Michigan's United States Senator Philip Hart and wife Jane (Briggs) Hart owned this cottage in the mid 1950s. Senator Hart was the former lieutenant governor of Michigan, serving under Governor G. Mennen Williams, who later owned a cottage on West Bluff (see West Bluff Cottage 4).

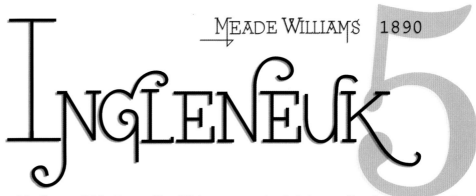

INGLENEUK

MEADE WILLIAMS 1890

"Rev. Meade Williams and family of St. Louis are here again for the season. Mr. Williams is the author of 'Early Mackinac' a book well known, especially to the resorting people. His son Jesse Lynch Williams has also made a name of wide spread fame as the author of the famous 'Princeton Stories'".

Daily Resorter, July 1901

Rev. Meade C. Williams, a native of Ft. Wayne, Indiana, who later lived in St. Louis, Missouri, expressed his great affection for Mackinac Island through his books. The first, *The Old Mission Church of Mackinac Island,* is a twenty-two page church history written in 1895,

presumably from within the walls of this cottage. Rev. Williams' preservation efforts helped save the historic Old Mission Church, where he often preached as

a guest minister on Sundays during the summer months. Williams wrote another book in 1897, *Early Mackinac: A Sketch Historical and Descriptive*, which he revised in 1901 and 1912. In 1986, a Michigan publisher reprinted it, making it a standard regional book on the shelves of local bookstores and in the private homes of Mackinac Island enthusiasts.

Meade C. Williams' father, Jesse Lynch Williams, is noted as a Ft. Wayne pioneer. Jesse Lynch Williams is also the name given to Meade C. Williams' son who wrote a preface for the 1986 reprint of *Early Mackinac: A Sketch Historical and Descriptive.*

Meade's brother Henry Williams married Mary Hamilton whose brother Montgomery Hamilton owned a cottage nearby (see East Bluff Cottage 14).

6 MONTEZUMA
1890–1891 · EZRA BARNARD

"Montezuma is the Mexican sobriquet of E. P. Barnard's literally 'way-up.'"

Daily Resorter, July 28, 1894

Ezra Perry Barnard, his wife, and two daughters, Mary and Isabel, had a cottage built here in 1890. Two years later, they completely remodeled it into a Shingle Style summer cottage. The exterior wall surface is covered with wooden shingles flowing with the roof surface so it is seemingly connected and continuous. The original arched openings of the recessed porch allowed the cool breeze off the water to refresh the cottage inhabitants, even on the hottest summer days.

Barnard learned the lumbering trade from his father, a part-time farmer in the summer and part-time lumberman in the winter. At age 14, Ezra left New York and headed west, looking for work. He reached Detroit in 1848. He got the notion to explore further so he walked across Michigan to White Lake, a distance of 157 miles, to find a job working a raft down the Flat River near Greenville. In 1854, he assisted in building one of the first circular mills in the country. He later sold his interest in that business to contract with a new railroad, the Detroit, Grand Haven & Milwaukee, to provide pilings for tracks around Fruitport and Spring Lake.

Adventure moved him to take a schooner to Chicago where he boarded the first train headed west. A Nebraska cattleman employed most of the passengers and Ezra needed a job so he signed on. The job was herding cattle from Nebraska to Salt Lake City. At the end of the drive, he and six others bought "two yoke of cattle," continuing their journey across the Rocky Mountains to California. There he set up his circular saw and prospered by cutting down the sugar pine trees of that region. He returned home to form a partnership with James Stewart on the Flat River and operated his ever-improving circular saw, moving to successive locations as he depleted each site's standing timber. He culminated his milling operations in 1887 in Menominee in Michigan's Upper Peninsula, where his saw milled 30,000,000 feet of lumber and 5,000,000 shingles per year. He operated this mill until 1893, when he retired in Detroit. It is not surprising that Ezra Barnard built a wooden Shingle Style cottage.

In 1899, Montezuma had new owners, Johann Buehler and wife Rose (Schoppe) of Chicago. They had two children, John William, Jr. and Louisa. In Chicago, Buehler owned a malt house and from 1874 until 1878, served as an Illinois state senator. The next owners, in 1907, were the Hitchcock family from Muncie, Indiana, who sold their cottage on Huron Street to move to this East Bluff location. (See Lakeshore Cottage 9).

7 YONONTE

JOHN and LIDA ATKINSON

1885

"Colonel Atkinson, of Detroit, has leased a lot at National Park and will build a $2,000 cottage this fall."

Daily Resorter, July 28, 1894

Island carpenter Alfred G. Couchois built this cottage for $2,000 in 1885. The cottage name, Yononte, derives from the Portuguese phrase, *no monte*, meaning "on the hill."

Detroit attorney John Atkinson and his wife Lida (Lyons) Atkinson brought the popular East Coast architectural style known as Shingle Style to Mackinac Island. An open wrap-around porch terminating in a balustraded balcony and an octagonal belvedere afforded the occupants of the cottage unparalleled views of the Straits of Mackinac and daily steamship arrivals. Inside, the main living room runs the full width of the house.

In 1887, the cottage changed hands to new owners, the decorated veteran of the Civil War and Spanish American War, General Henry Martyn Duffield of Detroit, Michigan and his wife Francis Pitt, whose ancestors sailed on the Mayflower. The Duffields had six sons, Henry, Divie B., Francis, and Graham (see East Bluff Cottage 16), who remained in Detroit, and Morse and Pitts who lived in Salt Lake City and New York respectively.

General Duffield's military career began with his enlistment in the 9th Michigan Infantry in 1861. Henry's older brother, Col. William Ward Duffield, commanded the unit. Henry mustered in as quartermaster. In one month, Henry achieved the rank of first lieutenant, then made colonel in 1864. William and Henry stayed together through most of the Civil War. Both brothers were taken prisoner of war during the Battle of Stones River in Murfreesboro, Tennessee. A third brother, Rev. Samuel Duffield, was also a Civil War soldier.

Following Henry's discharge from the Army, he was admitted to the Michigan bar and practiced law from 1865 to 1898. Then, the cry of battle rose again during the Spanish American War, and Duffield earned the title brigadier general in charge of volunteers. He achieved the rank of major general in 1903. A year later General Duffield sold the Mackinac Island cottage, two years before his wife's death. He died in Detroit in 1912 at the age of seventy.

Buena Vista

TILESTON AND MARY SPANGLER

1891

The beautiful view has not changed since T. F. and Mary Spangler had their cottage built on this lot in 1891. Stairs wind in two flights to the covered wraparound front porch of this lovely structure. Its gable roof dormer is ornamented with a scroll sawn clover leaf pattern cutout. A sawtooth vergeboard edges the second floor eaves, complementing the imbricated shingles of the exterior walls. The wood shingles on the first floor's exterior, inspired by the popular East Coast Shingle Style cottage, were readily available to builders in northern Michigan and very popular.

Zanesville, Ohio, claimed Colonel T. F. Spangler as one of its leading citizens in 1867. He taught high school there for two years after graduation. In 1870 he studied law and was admitted to the Ohio bar in 1873. Spangler decided to apply his legal training to banking and real estate. To further his real estate interest, he established the firm of Spangler & Finley, which lasted from 1881 to 1887. He laid out the towns of Fair Oaks, Brighton, Maplewood, and Tiledale.

In 1883, Ohio Governor George Hoadley commissioned Spangler as a military staff aide with the rank of colonel. He served in that capacity for two

years, performing military service for ten days during the Cincinnati riot. After the next election, newly-elected Governor James Campbell re-appointed Spangler to the same position.

Spangler married Mary Sullivan Cox with whom he had four children, Leola, Dorothea, Helen, and Arthur. Mary was the sister of a well-known writer and newspaper editor, Samuel "Sunset" Cox. Spangler's second wife was Mary Buckingham Green.

In addition to teaching and practicing law, Spangler founded the People's Saving Bank two years prior to building this Mackinac Island cottage. Spangler was a multi-talented and very busy individual. Aside from his other endeavors, he directed the local workhouse, served as an officer in civic and professional organizations, and was an elder in his church. After all this it is amazing that Spangler still had time to enjoy this lovely cottage.

Spangler was interested in architecture as well as real estate. Following frequent travels to other countries, he returned home and reproduced the pagodas, porticos or bridges seen on his most recent journey and placed them in Spangler Park, his private estate in Zanesville.

Like the other cottages in the tour, this lovely cottage is private property. Please respect the occupant's privacy and do not trespass.

9 FAR VIEW

1892   HENRY JENNESS

Henry and Lillis Jenness displayed their fine taste in architecture by hiring Mason and Rice, architects of the Grand Hotel, to design their home in Detroit. On the Island, they contracted with local builder Mathias Elliott to erect this unusual Shingle Style cottage in 1892. Rising from a rubblestone base, this very private gable roof cottage is flanked with a conical roof porch enclosed with multi-paned windows. A conical roof dormer projects from the second story. The free-flowing plan with a porch is loosely arranged around a great hall. Mathias Elliott also built the Taylor, Freeman, Spangler and Batten cottages on East Bluff. He charged about $1,500 to build his designs.

Henry Leland Jenness, described in *The Detroit Free Press* as a capitalist, acquired a profitable business in Detroit selling crockery, china, and bronzed lamps. He specialized in fruit jars, lamp materials, and American crockery and also practiced law. Henry and Lillis had one child, a daughter Constance Burt. On the Island, Lillis must have had great times with her sisters, Mrs. C. Van Cleve Ganson, (see East Bluff Cottage 11) and Sarah Fisher, (see East Bluff Cottage 4), who also owned East Bluff cottages. When Lillis was back in Detroit, she volunteered for church and charity work at the Woodward Avenue Baptist Church and the Protestant Orphan Asylum.

Beginning in 1905, Far View's next owners were Frank Dinsmore and his wife Mary Campbell. They had three children: Mrs. Harold Comey, Joseph C., and Campbell. Dinsmore, an attorney, was an official with

"H. L. Jenness, a prominent attorney of Detroit together with Mrs. Jenness and daughter, Constance arrived at their cottage Far View."

Daily Resorter, July 17, 1893

Proctor and Gamble. His most noted accomplishment was his thirty-year service on the University of Cincinnati Board of Directors.

Mrs. Dinsmore loved this cottage and its wonderful gardens. The Dinsmores held title to the cottage until 1955, when Milton and Lillian Tootle's granddaughter, Katherine Tootle Hannabass, acquired the dwelling.

credit Mackinac State Historic Parks, Michigan

27

10 TOOTLE COTTAGE
MILTON and LILLIAN TOOTLE   1900

Milton, Jr. and Lillian (Duckworth) Tootle hired local builder Patrick Doud for this building project in 1900. Doud's first job was demolishing and hauling away General G. W. Smith's cottage that contractor Charles Caskey had built on this lot in 1888. The cottage Doud erected is one of the most distinctive on the Island. Designed in the same style as the Tootle mansion in St. Joseph, Missouri, it resembles a sandstone castle on the Rhine.

The family's fortune came from Milton, Sr. and Catherine (O'Neill) Tootle, whose merchandise outlet outfitted gold-panners and pioneer settlers of the western frontier. Tootle's success prompted Chicago's Marshall Field to comment, "I hope I may someday have as fine a wholesale business as Mr. Tootle has." Milton Tootle, Sr. even founded a town of his own, Miltonvale, Kansas, where the Tootlefest is held every year in August.

Milton, Jr. was only fifteen years old when his father died, but when he was of age, he managed to fill his father's shoes. He continued the established business ventures and also explored interests of his own, such as landscape design and architecture. He became vice president of Tootle-Lemon National Bank, a business organized by his Uncle Thomas. He inherited the majestic Tootle Theatre that his father built in 1871, and had it remodeled in 1893. He served as director of the Tootle, Wheeler & Motter Mercantile Company, later known as Tootle-Campbell Drygoods Company, one of the strongest and most widely known jobbing houses in the Midwest. He was president of the Tootle-Kessler Millinery Company, vice-president of the Buell Woolen Mills, and president of the Tootle Estate, which held large interests in the Aunt Jemima Mills Company. He married Lillian Bell Duckworth when he was twenty years old, and they had three sons: Milton, Duckworth, and William.

Milton Tootle, Jr. enjoyed his leisure time on the Island and spent it in pursuit of his love of gardening. He hired landscape architect T. R. Otsuka to design terraced gardens with tiny miniature fountains and

waterfalls. Small trees were trained with unlimited patience to resemble sailboats or other desired shapes.

Milton Tootle, Jr.'s granddaughter, Katherine Hannabass, first visited the Island at three weeks old in the arms of her father. After seventy years of summering on the island, she recalled her grandfather spending most of his day in the garden, only breaking for lunch announced by Mrs. Tootle's bell. After lunch he returned to the garden. Old photos show garden trails and a teahouse, which do not survive. But many of the trees and plants from Tootle's landscaping efforts do survive and flourish, on this lot and also on neighboring lots. The unusual one hundred-year-old trees on the front lawn are Camperdown Elm, a grafted tree also known as Umbrella Elm or Weeping Elm. This variety of tree originated from a seedling at Camperdown House, near Dundee, Scotland and is a cultivar of the Scotch Elm. The leaves show a high degree of asymmetry at the base and are dark green in color. The drooping branches have made it attractive as a small-scale landscaping tree.

A comparison of the current photo with the one taken between 1900 and 1925, reveals the addition of a two-story Ionic order porch with railings and leaded glass windows. The grandeur of this distinctive summer cottage, held by the Tootle family for fifty years, has not diminished over the century.

DOLCE DOMUM

SAMUEL & PHEBE GEHR

credit Mackinac State Historic Parks, Michigan

Dolce Domum is distinguished as the first cottage built on land leased in the National Park. The cottage has changed very little since 1885 except for the red roof installed in 1946. It remains the simple Carpenter Gothic built by Charles Caskey over one hundred years ago.

Phebe Bostock married Samuel H. Gehr in 1857, in Chicago, where he moved after attending Marshall College in Pennsylvania. He studied for the bar but never practiced law. Instead he applied his legal

"Mrs. S. H. Gehr and Mrs. C. R. Warren of Chicago have each erected beautiful cottages on the National park east of the fort and are occupying them with their families and are enjoying themselves to the full extent of the law."

Daily Resorter, August 29, 1885

education to Chicago real estate. Phebe and Samuel had five children: S. Whipple, Herbert Bostock, Fannie, Francis Sycett, and Arthur, who joined his father's business in 1885. Arthur obtained a lease from the Park for an East Bluff lot but forfeited the lease and never built a cottage there.

A year after Samuel and Phebe built their cottage, Mr. Gehr fell victim to a stroke in their home, in Evanston, Illinois. The family thought the fresh air and sunshine of their Mackinac Island cottage would help him recover, so they placed him onboard the steamer *City of Duluth* bound for the Island. He was unconscious for the entire trip except for one brief interval. On arrival at the dock, the carriage delivered him to his doorstep. He drew his last breath at his Island home.

Other cottagers on East Bluff were Gehr's friends from Chicago and present at his funeral. Edward Hosmer had leased land in 1886, but forfeited the lease. John Batten built Sunrise, a neighboring cottage. General G.

W. Smith was the owner of a cottage once occupying the site of the Tootle Cottage. Gehr's character traits are documented in a speech given to the Chicago Board of Realtors upon his death: "His judgment and integrity have made casual customers steady clients and caused the name of Samuel Gehr to be classed with the real estate aristocracy of Chicago."

In 1898, C. Van Cleve Ganson from Grand Rapids, Michigan began to spend the summer months here at his newly purchased cottage. His wife's sisters, Lillis Jenness, who owned Far View cottage a few doors down, and Sarah Fisher who owned the Fisher Cottage influenced the acquisition.

Ganson practiced law for a number of years before he became involved with the merger of the Grand Rapids & Indiana Railroad and the Pennsylvania Railroad around 1898. Later, Mr. Ganson became interested in the real estate business.

CHARLOTTE WARREN & CHARLES BOWEN
WARREN COTTAGE
1885 & 1895

John Esaias Warren was a diplomat, lawyer, travel writer, real estate investor, and mayor of St. Paul, Minnesota. He married Charlotte Warren. Their two children, Mary N. "Nina" and Paul were born in Minnesota. The family moved to Chicago in 1867 where John engaged in the real estate business. His travel writing produced, "Tropics of the Times," "Para; or Scenes and Adventures on the Banks of the Amazon," and "Vagamundo; or The Attache in Spain." He took up residence in Brussels, Belgium a year after building their small Carpenter Gothic cottage next to the Gehrs. He died in Brussels in 1896. The cottage sold the year before to Charles C. Bowen of Detroit.

Charles Bowen converted the simple Caskey designed cottage into an elaborate double house connected by a giant Ionic portico. Two dramatic semicircular projections run the entire breadth of the two separate houses. A T-shaped house on the west, built by Charles Caskey, was probably the original cottage occupied by Charlotte and John Warren. Another gabled structure on the east was connected to form one stately Beaux Arts Classical dwelling.

Bowen, his wife, and three children, Lem, Caroline, and Adelaide, summered together for only a few seasons before Charles died in 1900. A generous man, he bequeathed valuable shares of D. M. Ferry Seed Company stock to his wife and children and endowed a $50,000 Greek professorship at Kalamazoo College. In appreciation of his generosity, Kalamazoo College named a classroom building Bowen Hall.

Owen Cottage

John and Jane Owen   1887

John and Jane (Cook) Owen had eight children, four of whom survived childhood: Edmund J.; Lafayette; John, Jr.; and Fannie Lathrop. John Owen died in 1891 just four years after building this cottage, and Jane Owen passed away in 1908.

John began a career in Detroit that parallels the history of banking and shipping in Michigan. In 1818, his widowed mother, looking for opportunity, moved to frontier Detroit. John began working as an errand boy for Dr. Chapin's Drug Store. When he was twenty years old, he became a partner in the business known as J. Owen & Company. While operating his store, he invested heavily in the Detroit & Cleveland Steam Navigation Company, ultimately serving as its president. This steamship line was a major player in transporting travelers to Mackinac Island. As a necessity for the steamship line, Owen organized the Detroit Dry Dock Company, of which he also became president.

As early as 1837, the year Michigan became a State, John Owen served as president of the Michigan Temperance Society, and he "ever labored for the obliteration of the liquor traffic in whatever guise presented."

In banking Mr. Owen took the helm of the Michigan Insurance Bank and National Insurance Bank, which soon became the First National Bank. In 1860, he was elected to the office of State Treasurer, serving during the Civil War years. His commitment to education found him a seat on the Board of Regents of The University of Michigan and Detroit College of Medicine. He served as a trustee of Albion College.

Following Owen's death, son John, Jr. managed the estate of his parents, but fell while riding horseback on Mackinac Island and died in 1924. His sister, Fannie Owen Lathrop, wanted a cottage of her own following her marriage, and chose to spend the summer season in the Captain's Quarters Cottage near the Fort. She remained in that cottage for a number of seasons before moving to the Morrison Cottage (see East Bluff Cottage 17) in 1900.

Originally built in the Shingle Style, the Owen cottage retains its rounded conical roof, engaged corner tower and its neat continuous horizontal flow. The third floor dormer that projects from the hip roof is capped with an extending quarter-round roof protecting the ribbon windows from the sun's glare or the rain's splatters. The defining elements of this lovely cottage have been retained through all remodeling projects.

14 1888 HAMILTON COTTAGE

MONTGOMERY & GERTRUDE HAMILTON

Montgomery and Gertrude (Pond) Hamilton built this cottage in 1888, three years after Mr. Hamilton dissolved a failed wholesale grocery business and partnership in Ft. Wayne, Indiana. He was active in the Democratic Party in the 1870s and 1880s and served on the Ft. Wayne City Council. He was director of the Hamilton National Bank, a venture of his father's undertaking.

The most notable success of the Hamiltons came through their five children, Edith, Alice, Margaret, Norah, and Arthur (nicknamed Quint). Edith and Alice are nationally renowned in their fields. Edith Hamilton, author of classic books on Greek and Roman mythology which she wrote after age fifty-four, retired as headmistress of Bryn Mawr School in 1922. Her phenomenal career as a writer gave the world *The Greek Way* and *Mythology*, which together sold almost three million copies.

Alice graduated from The University of Michigan Medical School in 1893 and began investigating diseases related to industrial occupations. She and her cousin Agnes worked with the famous social activist Jane Addams at Hull House in Chicago, improving the living conditions of the poor. Alice became a Harvard Medical School professor, the first female to hold this position.

It did not include the full faculty benefits enjoyed by the other male professors. She was barred from entering the Harvard Club, from marching in commencement, and from claiming her quota of football tickets! But she remained at Harvard as an assistant professor and published three books on Industrial Health. Her book, *Exploring the Dangerous Trades*, is an autobiography and also documents the specialty she introduced, Industrial Medicine.

In 1984, many of Alice's letters to family and friends were published in the book *Alice Hamilton: A Life in Letters*. Her letters about the Island expressed her strong affection for it. She penned the following, "During my childhood it was still untouched by modern progress, by the hideous architecture of the eighties and nineties…When I was ten we began to go to Mackinac Island, which became our summer home for many years…Wind in pine trees, water lapping on pebbly beach, I have heard them in Switzerland and in Bavaria and in Sicily, and always Mackinac has come sweeping back to me and I think it always will."

Alice is well respected nationwide. In 1995, the U.S. Postal Service issued a fifty-five cent stamp honoring Alice Hamilton, M.D. as part of the Great American stamp series.

Margaret followed in Edith's footsteps and taught school, becoming acting headmistress at Bryn Mawr College. Sister Norah studied at the Art Student's League in New York with James McNeil Whistler and went on to illustrate several of Jane Addams' books as well as her sister's autobiography.

Arthur was nicknamed Quint or Quintus by his sisters after a neighbor suggested in jest that Arthur be called "Primus." He became a popular teacher of French and Spanish at the University of Illinois at Urbana. He also wrote books on grammar and manners. He was the only one of the five children to marry, but he had no children.

The extended family included other cottagers and accomplished people.

"This is the sixth season for Mr. Montgomery and family of Ft. Wayne, Ind. Misses Edith and Marguerite and Master Arthur are all here to remain till September 1st . Mr. and Mrs. Hamilton's nieces, Misses Catherine and Josie and nephew Taber will spend the season with them."

Daily Resorter, July 17, 1893

above: Alice Hamilton Stamp credit United States Postal Service

Montgomery Hamilton's brother, Henry, married Meade C. Williams' sister (see East Bluff Cottage 5). Montgomery's brother, Andrew and wife, Phoebe, bought the Morrison cottage (see East Bluff Cottage 17) in 1924. The Hamiltons' niece, Agnes, in addition to her social work at Hull House, was an amateur artist who helped found the Ft. Wayne Art School.

She painted many scenes of Mackinac Island, now in the hands of private collectors.

Life size statues of Agnes, Edith, and Alice Hamilton stand in Ft. Wayne's Headwater Park in tribute to full lives, well lived. Edith died at age ninety-eight and Alice at 101 years old.

The cottage Alice referred to as "the homely little cottage" her father built on Mackinac Island is a typical Charles Caskey cross-gable design with wrap-around porch, reached by a broad flight of center stairs.

Bursley Cottage
Gilbert and Ellen Bursley   1890

"G.E. Bursley, wholesale grocer of Ft. Wayne, Indiana, his pleasant wife and two sons, Joseph A. and Phillip E., came several days ago."

Daily Resorter, July 17, 1893

Gilbert Bursley was a wholesaler, railroad superintendent, and business manager from Ft. Wayne, Indiana. Bursley, born in Barnstable, Massachusetts, left home at sixteen to find his first job at a Boston bookstore. From there, he worked for Old Colony Railroad and in 1862, enlisted in the Union Army's 130th New York Infantry. After the Civil War, he made Ft. Wayne, Indiana his home and was instrumental in organizing the Citizens Street Railroad Company. He supervised it for ten years. Bursley married Kate Smith, but she died ten years later, in 1871. In 1876, he met and married Ellen Rebecca Aldrich, and they had two sons, Joseph Aldrich and Philip Everett.

He was a member of the Ft. Wayne contingent who summered together on East Bluff, including Stephen B. Bond (see East Bluff Cottage 19), Montgomery Hamilton (see East Bluff Cottage 18), and R. S. Taylor (see East Bluff Cottage 22). They were all neighbors or business associates with either the Packard Piano Company of Ft. Wayne, Indiana or Hamilton's wholesale grocery business. Bursley was business manager and secretary of the piano company for ten years while Stephen Bond served as its president. Back in Ft. Wayne, Bursley, Bond, and Taylor all lived in the 300 block of Fairfield Avenue, evidence of their friendship as well as their business acquaintance.

G. E. Bursley's grandson was a high profile Michigan man. Gilbert E. Bursley, II, was a state senator, foreign diplomat, and Cleary College president. He was elected as state senator in 1960, was re-elected, and served until 1978. He died in Ann Arbor, Michigan in 1998. Bursley Hall on the campus of The University of Michigan is named in his honor.

16 CRAIG MAWR

MARY and JAMES WALSH   1890 - 1891

Twin-towered Craig Mawr, a Scottish name meaning high bluff, dwarfs its neighbors in the same way that it did when it was built in 1890. It occupies 6,500 square feet, contains nine bedrooms, four baths, and a contoured glass-wrapped front porch, perfect for watching the passing freighters.

The first owners of this cottage needed space for seven children and four servants, all making the jaunt from Chicago. Mary E. Walsh, daughter of Elizabeth and James Sheahan, long-time editorial writer at *The Chicago Tribune*, married Irish born James Walsh. James succeeded in the railroad business, serving as vice president of the Chicago & Southern Railway and later the Baltimore & Ohio Railway.

In 1890, the children: Adelaide, 15; Vincent, 13; Grosbeck, 12; Mildred, 9; Elizabeth, 7; Constance, 4; and Dorothy, 1, spent the summers exploring the lanes and paths of Mackinac Island on ponies or foot, often playing with other children their ages. These early friendships would deepen, at it did for son Vincent and his future wife, Julia Cudahy, daughter of John and Mary Cudahy (see West Bluff Cottage 4). Vincent became an attorney in Chicago, but died at age thirty-eight leaving no children. One of the other daughters married Graham Duffield, son of General and Francis Duffield (see East Bluff Cottage 7). Another daughter married Ralph Bond, son of Stephen and Jessie Bond (see East Bluff Cottage 19).

Adelaide, the oldest daughter, remained single and was at her mother's side in 1918 when she died. Grosbeck, a physician, practiced in the Panama Canal Zone in the early 1900s, returning home to continue his practice, conduct research, and publish many medical papers. The family held the cottage until 1922.

"Cottage receptions are one of the pleasantest features of life at the Island and one of the especially delightful events of the particularly pleasant features was the reception given this afternoon by Mrs. James Walsh of Chicago in honor of her daughter Miss Adelaide Walsh. The affair took place at the handsome Walsh cottage on the bluff. It lasted 4 to 6 and during the 2 hours many of Miss Walsh's young friends at the Grand and from the cottages were handsomely entertained. "

Daily Resorter, August 18, 1893

17 ANNE MORRISON MORRISON COTTAGE

1891

When Anne Morrison had this cottage built in 1891, she was the oldest of the three children born to Mary and Robert Morrison of Delaware, Ohio, and had never married. Her mother, Mrs. Mary Morrison, was widowed by 1890, and already seventy-three years old. Mary and Robert had daughters Mary L. and Anne, and a son James R., who became a civil engineer. The family lived comfortably at the corner of Washington and Griswold in Delaware, Ohio, attended by a live-in servant, Fred Day.

The Morrisons kept the cottage on Mackinac until 1900 when they sold it to Fannie Owen Lathrop, widow of George Howard Lathrop, and daughter of Jane and John Owen (see East Bluff Cottage 13). Mrs. Lathrop knew the Island well. She had summered at her parents' cottage, then later as an adult, had leased the Fort's Captain's Quarters as a summer cottage. Mrs. Lathrop was granted a reduction of $250 from the first year's rent of $350 due to her remodeling efforts.

The families who summered here found opportunities to share their discovery of Mackinac with cousins, uncles, and friends. The connection of people in the cottage community is evident with each house's history, and this one is no exception. Montgomery Hamilton's (see East Bluff Cottage 14) sister-in-law, Phoebe Hamilton, acquired the lease of the Morrison Cottage in the mid-1920s. After that time, the cottage fell into neglect and was forfeited to the Mackinac Island State Park.

Judge Robert Taylor had this two-story wood frame and shingle clad dwelling built by Mathias Elliott in 1892. His Ft. Wayne friends and fellow cottagers, Bond, Bursley, and Hamilton no doubt convinced him that the view and the companionship were worth the long trip from Indiana each summer.

Taylor was born in 1838 near Chillicothe, Ohio, the son of Rev. Isaac N. and Margaretta Steward Taylor, who founded Liber College near Portland, Indiana. Robert S. Taylor attended Liber College where he met classmate Fanny W. Wright. They married after he received his diploma in 1858. He practiced law in Ft. Wayne in 1866, forming the partnership of Ninde, Taylor, and Robertson. Ninde is noted for his participation in the Underground Railroad. In 1868, Taylor became prosecuting attorney and later, judge of the Court of Common Pleas. He capped off his career by serving Indiana's state legislature as a representative. Judge Taylor and Fanny had one son, Frank B. Taylor, who became a geologist studying postglacial geology of the Great Lakes.

The cottage underwent changes early in its history and also in the mid-

1930s, as is evident from the date 1931 written on a cellar beam. The subsequent remodeling project doubled the cottage size and created a balance of two identical but connected halves. This cottage was one of four on East Bluff erected by builder Mathias Elliot.

John J. and Katherine Tootle (see East Bluff Cottage 9) of St. Joseph, Missouri, owned this cottage from the 1920s until the 1960s.

19 BOND COTTAGE
STEPHEN BOND
1893

In 1887, the Ft. Wayne city directory lists Stephen Bond as president of the Old National Bank, president of the Ft. Wayne Organ Company (later the called the Packard Piano Company), and vice president of the Citizens Railroad Company. He is also listed as a cashier with Allen Hamilton & Company, a banking institution in Ft. Wayne headed by the father of Montgomery Hamilton, neighbor on the East Bluff. Bond and Hamilton were stockholders in the Sentinel Publishing Company. Stephen Bond was largely instrumental in building the street railway system of Ft. Wayne with fellow cottager and Ft. Wayne neighbor Gilbert E. Bursley.

Bond's financial success started with meager beginnings in 1848 when young Stephen was hired as a porter and assistant clerk in the Fort Wayne branch of the State Bank of Indiana. Five years later, he accepted a partnership in the Allen Hamilton & Company private bank. Jesse L. Williams, father of East Bluff cottager Rev. Meade Williams, was also a partner in this bank. Stephen and his brother, H. W. Bond, were associated in a sandstone quarry in Michigan that supplied the materials for many Ft. Wayne buildings.

On New Year's Day in 1863, Stephen Bond married Jessie M. Vermilyen, daughter of a Ft. Wayne innkeeper. They had nine children: Albert, Herbert, S. Charles, Frank D., Ralph (see East Bluff Cottage 16), Mrs. J. M. Kuhns, Mrs. Frank Brown, Miss Louise Bond, and Mrs. Edwin Evans of Toledo, Ohio.

Between 1910 and 1920, the cottage changed hands until it finally came under the ownership of Mrs. Metella Eckhardt. She fell on hard times and was faced with foreclosure when she could not come up with the required annual rent of $150. Refusing to give up the cottage, she pleaded before the park commission to stop the foreclosure, because she explained, "...she was blessed with second sight, and that when she first saw the house, she could see her father on the porch." She was allowed to stay and the rent was reduced to $25 a year.

This secluded cottage is the first of the East Bluff cottages to see the morning light, hence its name, Sunrise Cottage. Visitors should respect the privacy of the owners and stay on the walkway. The best view of this cottage is from the photograph.

John Batten was born in London, England in 1850 and came to the United States when he was four years old. He chose the law as his occupation, established a private practice, and was twice elected state's attorney for Du Page County, Illinois. In 1899, Batten was selected as judge of Cook County Probate Court.

In 1874, he married Ida Haight. They had three children: Marion, who married Albert Hayes Wetten; Percy Haight, a mechanical engineer in the em-

John and Ida Batten 1892
Sunrise 20

ploy of the Chicago & North Western Railway Company; and Ralph Ellsworth, an attorney who graduated from The University of Michigan Law School.

In the early 1900s, the cottage was transferred to Batten's son-in-law, Albert Hayes Wetten, who developed the largest real estate brokerage firm in Chicago. Albert secretly wanted to be a cartoonist and practiced his art in his early twenties,

abandoning it when he found the lucrative career in real estate. Joseph W. Cremin is listed on the lease with Wetten. Cremin was also in the real estate business in Chicago and served on the Chicago Real Estate Board with Wetten.

"At the extreme eastern end of the Island is 'Sunrise Cottage' owned by Mr. John H. Batten of Chicago. You pass what seems to be the last in this row on the east side, wander irresolutely around an alluring bend in the road where the lake gleams through the trees, where the primeval perfumes the air with woodsy fragrance on each side and follow another undulation of the roadway and another until the blue of the waters open full before you a crazy little rustic stairway turns and twists up, up, and up at the left and you find yourself on the eastern most peak of the Island, crowned by 'Sunrise Cottage' where old Sol certainly has every chance in the world to rout the inhabitants there of from their downy couches very early indeed in his day's journey. The felicitous name was suggested to Mr. Batten by Mr. Franklin S. Hanson, of Chicago, whose own cottage near the extreme western end bears the equally appropriate name of 'Sunset Cottage.' It is a large home-like dwelling built in rustic style and one of the most popular resorting places on the Island."

Daily Resorter, July 28, 1894

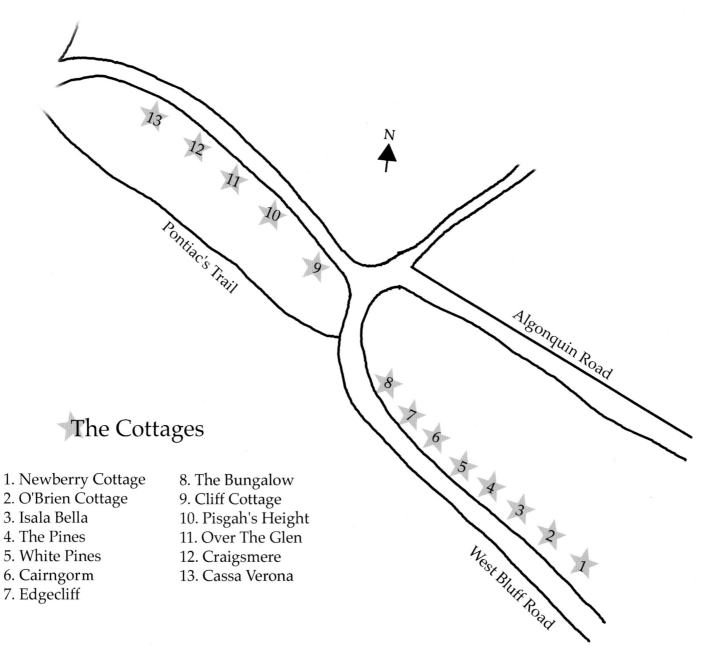

Mackinac Island
West Bluff

N

Pontiac's Trail

Algonquin Road

West Bluff Road

⭐ The Cottages

1. Newberry Cottage
2. O'Brien Cottage
3. Isala Bella
4. The Pines
5. White Pines
6. Cairngorm
7. Edgecliff
8. The Bungalow
9. Cliff Cottage
10. Pisgah's Height
11. Over The Glen
12. Craigsmere
13. Cassa Verona

WEST BLUFF

"The new electric lights are promised the west end cottages sometime next week. The poles are already placed and wiring will be completed in a few days."

Daily Resorter, July 19, 1901

Thirteen of the original sixteen cottages built between 1886 and 1893 survive and stand along the south-facing West Bluff. Seven are ornate Queen Anne cottages, dazzling the architectural pilgrim with displays of varied wall surfaces, irregular massing, towers, and, the most important feature for a resort cottage, wrap-around verandas. The cottages sit on leased lots, a continuous arrangement since 1885. Across the back alley, outbuildings provide shelter for carriages or horses and seem untouched by time. Some have been converted to living quarters, but all generally display the architectural details of its cottage.

The West Bluff cottages are arranged in sequence from east to west, beginning with the Newberry Cottage located next to the Grand Hotel, and finishing the West Bluff with Cassa Verona next to Hubbard's Annex.

1 NEWBERRY COTTAGE
WALTER AND HARRIET NEWBERRY 1888

Three families associated with the brewery business summered in this cottage through the years. The original owner, Walter Cass Newberry, peddled hops in Detroit and Chicago from 1857 until his retirement. Subsequent owner Julius Stroh took over his father, Bernhard Stroh's, brewery business in Detroit in the 1880s until his death in 1939. In 1937, Julius Stroh sold the cottage to his friend and business associate, Armin Rickel, who was owner and president of Rickel Malt Company of Detroit.

Newberry was "born into" the hops business. His father Amasa Newberry worked as the first New York Hops Inspector in 1828. Due to the enormous growth in the brewing business in the 1800s, Walter C. Newberry made a handsome living in business with his uncles, Oliver Newberry of Detroit, and Walter Loomis Newberry of Chicago. The success of this business led to other successful enterprises until the start of the Civil War when Newberry put business affairs on hold to enlist in the Union Army as a private. By the end of the war, he was brevetted a brigadier general for gallantry.

Upon discharge, and after a six year detour in Virginia to build a brewery that met with "stubborn resistance to native prejudice against malt liquor," he moved north to Chicago to resume business in the brewery supply trade.

An odd mixture of Newberry's occupations came about when President Cleveland appointed him Postmaster of Chicago in 1889, the year after this cottage was built. Two years later, Newberry became a congressman, joining other notable generals in Washington at that time. Walter and Harriet (DeGrout) Newberry found time each summer to travel to Mackinac Island with their daughters, Mary and Jessica.

The Newberrys enjoyed the cottage for nine years before selling it to the Bimm family of Dayton, Ohio, in 1897. A 1901 *Daily Resorter* introduced Mr. Bimm, *"Mr. Bimm is President and General Manager of the Pasteur Filter Co., manufacturers of a filter that is guaranteed to remove all germs as well as dirt and other impurities from any water."*

In 1913, Julius Stroh, brew master from Detroit, acquired the cottage and made many changes, most noticeable is the addition to the rear, doubling the cottage size. A stroll along the walkway provides a view of the cottage side gable projecting east from the main wing's hip roof. From a large veranda, portions of which are enclosed, the owners and their guests enjoy the views of the straits. The cottage sits on one of the choicest locations, next to the Grand Hotel.

O'BRIEN COTTAGE
Thomas and Delia O'Brien

"Hon. T. J. O'Brien and family of Grand Rapids general counsel of the G. R.& I have just arrived at their summer home near the Grand."

Daily Resorter, July 15, 1900

Thomas J. O'Brien played a pivotal role promoting the Grand Rapids & Indiana Railroad Company. He became director of the Mackinac Hotel Company, an organization responsible for building the Grand Hotel, providing a destination for his passengers.

His early education came in a country schoolhouse near his family's farm in Jackson County, Michigan. His high school education in Marshall, Michigan provided an opportunity to read law in the office of attorney John Fitzgerald. O'Brien was admitted to the bar in 1864. He formed a partnership with Fitzgerald until 1871, when he met D. Darwin Hughes, a leader of the bar in central Michigan and general counsel for the Grand Rapids & Indiana Railroad Company. Hughes saw a bright future in O'Brien and took him on as a partner to form a new firm, Hughes, O'Brien, & Smiley. The partnership terminated when Hughes died in 1883, at the height of the railroad expansion. O'Brien accepted an appointment as new general counsel of the G. R. & I.

In 1905, President Theodore Roosevelt appointed O'Brien to serve as ambassador to Denmark. Beginning in 1907, he served as ambassador to Japan for four years, and in 1911, President William Taft appointed him as ambassador to Italy.

Thomas and Delia (Howard) O'Brien had a son, Howard, and daughter, Katherine, who enjoyed this lovely little shingle-clad summer cottage. The two porches, on the first and second floors, one atop the other, allowed for views and breezes off the straits and for keeping an eye on the neighboring business interest, the Grand Hotel. The cottage is painted brown, a color from nature used by many early cottage owners.

The empty lot to the left is the site of William Hughart's cottage, built in 1888. Hughart was President of the Grand Rapids & Indiana Railroad. The cottage burned in 1978 and was not rebuilt.

I SALA BELLA

DELOS BLODGETT   1893

This Colonial Revival cottage boasts a gambrel roof wing projecting south from the main core of the shingled home. Its conical engaged round tower is toward the west. The open porches and balcony allow the occupants to enjoy the out of doors and mingle with nature.

Its original occupants were residents of Grand Rapids, Michigan. Delos A. Blodgett and his family of grown children, Susan and John, summered here following the 1890 death of their mother, Jennie (Wood) Blodgett. The Blodgetts had been married for thirty-one years. Delos remarried Miss Daisy Peck from Atlanta, Georgia in 1893. They had three children: Helen Blodgett Erwin; Delos A., Jr.; and Mona P. Guilland. As Helen Erwin later related, with a new stepmother, the older children had some concern regarding the family property. John spoke to Daisy of his sister's distress at the prospect of having her house taken away by her father's new bride. To settle the issue, Mr. Blodgett told Daisy if she wished to summer on Mackinac Island, she must choose another place. She could have her pick of any place she wanted, and so she selected a beautiful site up the hill and several blocks from the Grand Hotel (see West Bluff Cottage 13). Delos' daughter Susan, wife of Edward Lowe of Detroit, continued to enjoy the cottage until 1898 when it was sold to John Brittain of St. Louis, Missouri.

The Delos Blodgett story is one of a pioneer, lumberman, banker, and philanthropist, and sug-

gests the vigor of the American entrepreneurial spirit. Delos Abiel Blodgett began his career and fortune as an accountant and log scaler in a sawmill at little Bay de Noc, a village in Michigan's Upper Peninsula. He saw opportunity for wealth in the lumber industry. The subsequent history of this man, his family, and their Grand Rapids hometown turned on a small incident in 1847. Young Blodgett boarded the last vessel of the season from Racine, Wisconsin back to Bay de Noc to return to work. He suddenly discovered, while still docked at Racine, that someone had stolen his coat. He decided to track the thief,

following him to Milwaukee where he regained his belongings. But he could not find passage back to Bay de Noc, so he boarded a ship bound for Muskegon, Michigan, and found employment in a different lumber camp.

Young Blodgett gained a foothold in the forests at the headwaters of the Muskegon River. After further exploration by canoe, he and his partner, Thomas Stimson, found a tract of land that yield 600,000 board feet of lumber in the spring. The logs that were floated into Muskegon Lake that year launched an expanding operation. Blodgett founded the villages of Hersey and Evart by clearing the land of lumber and planting the first potato crop at his farm in Hersey. In 1881, Mr. Blodgett moved to Grand Rapids where he became one of the main stockholders in the Old Kent Saving Bank. John Wood Blodgett established The Blodgett Memorial Hospital in Grand Rapids as a tribute to his father, Delos Blodgett.

THE PINES

JOHN and MARGARET CUDAHY 1888

The Pines was built for the John Cudahy family of Chicago by architect Asbury Buckley in 1888, one of his most masterful accomplishments. This huge Shingle Style cottage is set on a stone wall foundation. The arched breezeway below the veranda diverts the wind to cool all four levels of the cottage. From the belvedere atop a square bedroom to the bell-roofed round towers rising above the structure, this splendid asymmetrical cottage is sheathed in wooden fish scale shingles. The lattice-work brings the detail together to give a unified round and smooth appearance. The sweeping curved veranda invites guests for lounging, laughter, and lemonade.

Among the cottage community on Mackinac Island, the Cudahy name is legendary. John Cudahy, one of five brothers, married twice. First, he married Mary Nolan, mother of Bessie and Julia, and later married Margaret F. O'Neill, mother of John R. and Gerald C. The flamboyant style of this family often made news in the *Daily Resorter*, that reported seeing the family motoring down the lake on their yacht, *Idler*, or shopping in the village for their frequent gatherings while their servants scurried about the cottage grounds, grooming the horses, or polishing the carriages. The Cudahy style of summer resort living was all financed from profits of their Chicago, Omaha, and Milwaukee meatpacking businesses.

John Cudahy was one of seven children born to Irish immigrants, Patrick and Elizabeth Cudahy. Emblematic of the classic immigrant story, the Cudahy family sailed from potato blight stricken Callan County, Kilkenny, Ireland, November 2, 1849, on the *Goodwind*, a coffin ship. The foreboding nickname proved a reality for John's infant sister, Anna, who died on the journey to America. John, Michael, Patrick, and their sister Catherine made the journey successfully. The family landed in Milwaukee, Wisconsin and lived there until Patrick, Sr. moved the family to Chicago where he found work in a brickyard. The family scraped by, but the sons were always looking for a way to improve their lot. They finally found an opportunity in the meatpacking business and took it.

"It was at this time of rapid expansion and change in the 1860s that the Cudahy boys started their careers in the meat packing industry," writes Joseph Kennedy, Cudahy descendent and author of *The Cudahys: an Irish American Success Story*. "They began in their teens toiling as laborers in slaughterhouses and meat plants and steadily worked their way up the ladder step by step. The whole industry was a mosaic of partnerships forming and

John Cudahy and family credit Mackinac State Historic Parks, Michigan

50

"Mr. and Mrs. John Cudahy, whose family and servants came last week were expected to arrive Wednesday."

Daily Resorter, July 1901

changing until it eventually sorted itself out. The Cudahys entered into this maelstrom with nothing more ambitious on their minds than getting steady employment. In a little over two decades, the boys rose to be captains of industry. Two of them, John and Patrick, Jr. were to start the Cudahy Brothers Packing Company in Milwaukee in 1888 while young Edward and his dynamic trail blazing brother, Michael, established one of the giants of the meat packing industry in 1890, the Cudahy Packing Company. The poor emigrants with only minimal education achieved prodigious success with only ambition and hard work."

But John Cudahy's confident and ambitious personality must have had a hand in his ability to take risks such as his financial finagling that completely wiped out his assets at one point when he tried to corner the market in pork and lard and lost four million dollars in 1893. He averted the disaster and regained his standing in the industry, recouping his losses (with help from his brothers), and gained another fortune to boot."John Cudahy's rise on the change has been one of the most pyrotechnically brilliant flashes of private financial history on record. He has made and lost millions upon millions and the present loss is not his first," reported the *Daily Resorter* on August 4, 1893.

Two of the other Cudahy brothers, Edward and Michael, enjoyed cottages on the Island as well. Michael reconstructed Francis Stockbridge's dwelling, Lakecliffe, a commodious cottage perched at the very edge of the Annex that housed its own billiard room (see Annex Cottage 19). Edward never built a cottage of his own, but bought his brother's Lakecliffe cottage. This transaction allowed Michael to travel and make a real estate deal in California, returning to Mackinac Island in 1904 to build the largest summer cottage on the Island, Stonecliffe (see Lakeshore Cottage 20). As their brother Patrick, Jr. wrote in his autobiography, "Poverty has been the making of many a prosperous man."

Its subsequent owners also distinguish The Pines Cottage. Eugene McDonald, founder of Zenith Radio Corporation, summered here with his family in the 1940s. Later, six-term Governor of Michigan, G. Mennen "Soapy" Williams and his wife Nancy acquired the cottage. Williams served as Michigan's governor from 1949 to 1961. During those years, they spent as much time at the Governor's Summer Residence as obligations of the office would allow. After his final term, Nancy and Soapy bought The Pines cottage, spending more than twenty-five years enjoying the view. Soapy is buried on Mackinac Island, the place he loved.

5 WHITE PINES

1887 DAVID and MARGARET HOGG

Originally built as a small cottage in 1887, it was remodeled in 1893 by architect and builder, Asbury Buckley into this Queen Anne cottage. White Pines and Cairngorm, Hannah's cottage next door, featured similar asymmetrical massing and architectural details: covered verandas, porches, towers, and balconies wrapped with diamond and fish scale shingles.

Cottage owner, David Hogg was born in Kinrossshire, Scotland, worked as a fresco painter and paperhanger in the eastern U.S., and came to Chicago in 1869. There he met fellow countryman, Alexander Hannah and formed the partnership of Hannah and Hogg in 1874. Together, they purchased fifty percent interest in James Stuart's Thistle Brand of liquor and started selling liquors and fine cigars in an increasing number of Chicago saloons. In 1874, the first was located at 190 W. Madison, then another at 188 W. Madison. By 1876, their saloons appeared up and down Madison, LaSalle, Randolph, and Monroe Streets. In the midst of all the business enterprise, David met and married Margaret Grady, in 1877. They had four children: Robert, Ethel (Mrs. L. R. Adams), Raymond, and Grace. Margaret enjoyed Mackinac Island summer with her sister Catherine Hannah (see West Bluff Cottage 6) who built a cottage next door.

"A.D. Hannah and family of Chicago are at Cairngorm and Mr. Hannah's partner, David Hogg, will be here soon; the latter's family however, came several days ago. The cottages of these two gentlemen are among the finest on the island."

Daily Resorter, July 17, 1893

David Hogg's White Pines is also pictured on p. 2 and p. 137

Remodeled from a modest cottage built in 1887, Cairngorm stands as majestically as it did when Asbury Buckley erected this Queen Anne for the Alexander Donnon Hannah family of Chicago in 1892. It features a prominent circular tower and wrap-around porch. Buckley also built the neighboring Queen Anne for Hannah's business partner, David Hogg. These cottages looked similar enough that a *Daily Resorter* newspaper report dubbed them "twin cottages" (see West Bluff Cottage 5).

Alexander Donnon Hannah came to the United States from Scotland with his parents and found his first job as a clerk in Kansas City, Missouri. In 1868, he moved to Chicago at the age of twenty-four where he met fellow countryman David Hogg, and joined in his liquor business, forming the partnership of Hannah and Hogg in 1873. They became an important entry in the saga of Chicago's booming saloon and distillery business. The successful liquor business financed a hotel purchase where they sold their wares in its saloon. The Hannah & Hogg Brevoort Hotel, shortened to Hotel Brevoort, was a Chicago landmark for many years. The label of Hannah and Hogg liquor still is available, known in the trade as bar liquor.

ALEXANDER & CATHERINE HANNAH
CAIRNGORM
1887 – 1888

Hannah and Hogg were in partnership together, built summer residences next to each other on Mackinac Island, and were neighbors on Oak Street in Chicago. They married sisters, Catherine and Margaret Grady, making them brothers-in-law as well.

Alexander married Catherine Grady. They had three children: Alexander W. (See Lakeshore Cottage 18); Mabel, who married Arthur McIntosh; and Hazel.

Alexander Hannah's Cairngorm is also pictured p. 137

7 EDGECLIFF

1886 WILLIAM and SARAH WESTOVER

William Westover, Jr. was from a prominent lumbering family in Bay City, Michigan. He built a small cottage on a National Park lot in 1886, the first cottage built on West Bluff. It survived about six years, changing hands twice before the Ambergs of Chicago acquired the land lease and tore down the old cottage. The Queen Anne that Asbury Buckley designed and built rises two-and-a-half stories, supports two corner towers, and is adorned with a frieze of swags across its exterior walls. The wrap-around veranda provides the guests welcome shade while they relax on wicker chairs and enjoy the sun's sparkle off the straits below.

William Amberg, born in Bavaria, saw the cottage construction completed in 1892. He named it Inselheim, German for "Island Home," but later changed the name to Edgecliff. He married Sarah Agnes Ward, and they had three children: John, Mary Agnes, and Genevieve.

Amberg's occupation was in the stationery business. He founded his own company, Cameron, Amberg & Company, only to have it destroyed by the Chicago Fire of 1871. Beginning again at a new location, the business was destroyed by another fire in 1878. Yet another new company, Amberg File & Index Company manufactured and distributed his invention, the file folder. In seven years, he acquired thirty patents and 600 copyrights pertaining to the file and indexing business. With money in the bank he branched out into the quarry business, putting Amberg, Wisconsin and Amberg granite on the map.

Back on Mackinac Island, Mr. Amberg's son, John, and fellow Annex cottager, Dr. L.L. McArthur, teamed up to build a six-hole "meadow" golf course in a cow pasture near the Annex (See Annex Cottages 8 and 9). After a few years, they negotiated for more land, establishing Wawashkamo Golf Club.

On most occasions, William and his son John were found perfecting their game on the golf course. Amberg loved the game and died after a round of golf. The cottage remained in the Amberg family until 1942.

Agnes Amberg Feidler, William Amberg's neice, returned to Mackinac on her ninetieth birthday in 1996 and shared her childhood memories at Edgecliff. She recalled, "In 1931, the family still had the cottage. Mrs. Amberg had hay fever. When they came to Mackinac they brought the horses, the help, the groomsman, lock, stock, and barrel."

"Will Westover has a cottage at Mackinaw Island on the high bluff on the north side and the only inconvenience about the place was the lack of good water. A long wire was stretched out in the lake to a distance of 500 feet from the foot of the bluff, the end being anchored by a large stone. This forms the track for a pail which is run down the incline of the wire. To the pail is attached a smaller wire which runs over a windlass and thus it is hoisted up filled with the fresh water of the straits."

The Bay County Tribune, 1886

"The Resorter representative was forcibly impressed by the magnificence of the new cottage of W. A. Amberg of Chicago. It will be occupied during the season by Mr. Amberg, his wife, daughter, and son. Mr. Amberg was formerly of the well-known firm of Cameron, Amberg and Co. of Chicago.."

Daily Resorter, July 17, 1893

THE BUNGALOW
1889 | WILLIAM GILBERT

William D. Gilbert, a relative of the Tootles (See East Bluff Cottage 10) was in the banking and lumber business in Grand Rapids, Michigan. He had a two-story Carpenter Gothic frame house with scroll sawn trim and a small front porch built in the shadow of the large Queen Anne dwellings dominating this bluff. The lovely 1889 cross-gabled cottage with its wrap-around porch survives in perfect form.

The lease records indicate the cottage was held in the estate of William Gilbert although his brother, Thomas Gilbert and wife Mary A. Bingham Gilbert, were the principal occupants. Mary held title from 1904 until 1940. She brings fame to this family of her own account as a poet and daughter of a famous missionary, Abel Bingham. Bingham operated his mission among the Ojibwa in Sault Ste. Marie, Michigan, providing fond memories for Mary. She continued her dedication and involvement in her father's mission among the Ojibwa until her death. Mary Gilbert enjoyed poetry and wrote under the *nom de plume* "Angie" Bingham. In Grand Rapids in 1886, she published a number of works, including a six-page Mackinac Island poem, "Devils Kitchen Mackinaw Island."

In an Island tradition, the cottage furniture is included with the sale of the cottage. True to form, the Gilbert's dining room table continues to serves its owners and their guests with the same hospitality provided over one hundred years ago.

Mary and Tom Gilbert credit Clarke Historical Library

"Atty. Geo. Cass of Chicago has purchased the cottage of Senator Leman. Mrs. Cass and two children are here for the season."

Daily Resorter, July 19, 1893

1888
CLIFF COTTAGE

HENRY & FRANCES LEMAN

9

This 1888 two-and-a-half story Queen Anne presents a front facing gable, recessed and multi-pane sash windows, and flared roof along with many permutations of roof lines and window treatments that add interest to this commodious cottage.

It was built for Chicago's Senator Henry Warren Leman and his wife, Frances E. (Dole) Leman who married in 1881. Their two children, Sheldon Dole and Frances M., enjoyed summers on the Island finding many neighboring playmates the same age.

Henry Leman attended law school but abandoned the practice to become vice president of the Chicago Title & Trust Company, a company he founded in 1890. Previously he had served a five year term as senator of the Sixth District of Illinois. He sold Cliff Cottage to George and Rebecca J. (Osborne) Cass of Chicago in 1893.

George, nephew of the first governor of the Michigan Territory, Lewis Cass, was an accomplished man of his own merit. He graduated with honors from Kenyon College, entered law school at The University of Michigan, and graduated in 1873. He moved to Louisville, Kentucky and headed up a railroad, the Pittsburgh, Fort Wayne & Chicago Railroad. He also managed a company named Adams Express in Louisville, Kentucky. Opportunities led him to move to Chicago. His interest in cricket attracted him to find ten other horsemen to found the Chicago Cricket Club in May 1876, and he may have practiced this sport on the Island.

Cass' son-in-law, William Shelby, great grandson of the first governor of Kentucky and new president of the Grand Rapids & Indiana Railroad, was next to hold title to the cottage. Shelby married Mary Kennedy Cass, George and Rebecca Cass' daughter. They held title to The Cliffs until 1908.

Other notables who held owned this cottage were Louis Swift, son of Chicago pioneer meatpacker, Gustavus Franklin Swift, and the Dixon family, also of Chicago, owners of Dixon Transfer Company.

"Mr. W. R. Shelby, President of the G.R. & I. Railroad has purchased the Cass Cottage on the West Bluff and was on the island yesterday looking it over besides incidentally caring for the interests of the railroad."

Daily Resorter, July 9, 1902

JOHN AND MARY EDGET

PISGAH'S HEIGHT

1890 – 1891

Mary and John Edget from Saginaw, Michigan built this unusual Shingle Style cottage in 1891. This frame house centers on its two-story bay. The wrap-around porch complements and unifies the dwelling.

Judge Edget began his law career at The University of Michigan School of Law, graduating in 1872. After a year of solo practice in Saginaw, he partnered with D. W. Perkins, and later with John Brooks. He served as city attorney for East Saginaw for three years and was interested in the consolidation of the Saginaws into one city. He was appointed district judge and held court from 1889 to 1893. Only his failing health prevented him from accepting a nomination as a justice on the Michigan Supreme Court. "The Winter Club" spoke of him as a genial and true friend who was true of character and purpose. He died at the age of forty-five at the Oak Grove Sanitarium in Flint, Michigan. John and Mary were able to spend only three seasons together in their cottage with their two daughters, Grace and Lucy.

Over the Glen

Thomas and Mary White   1889 – 1891

Grand Rapids lumberman Thomas Stewart White wanted to go to college but needed to earn money so he went to work instead. He got his feet wet in the lumber business after his father had bought some swampland at the head of Spring Lake near Grand Rapids, Michigan. His father asked Thomas to supervise cutting the timber. It was a taste of the woods that would linger and serve the family well, as White learned the trade the hard way, a $600 loss on that first deal.

In a lifelong career, he made millions off timber tracts of pine in Minnesota, cypress in New Orleans, and sugar pine in California. He sidelined in a Montana mine, Grand Rapids casting and stove manufacturing, and an Alabama iron works. When asked, in 1915, the cause of his success, he replied, "Being in so many things, we couldn't bust them all at once."

He married Mary E. Daniell of Milwaukee. They had five sons: Stewart Edward White, T. Gilbert, Rugee, Roderick, and Harwood. T. Gilbert was a noted painter and illustrator practicing his art in New York. Roderick became a concert violinist. Stewart Edward White achieved fame from his successful writing career which started with a pamphlet published by the Orthinologists Union titled, "Birds of Mackinac." He continued until thirty or forty adventure novels had been written and published. The influence of Mackinac Island and the lumber business are evident in the characters, adventures, and settings of Stewart Edward White's books. One of his early and most successful novels, *The Blazed Trail*, was written in 1902 while he worked in a lumber camp. He is often compared to his contemporary, Jack London. White's legacy has a permanent if not prominent place in the literary history of Michigan and the American West.

Over The Glen, built in 1890, is a two-and-a-half story Queen Anne with circular tower and wrap-around porch. The two-story barn behind the property supports a gable roof.

"Mrs. T. Stewart White of Grand Rapids calls her cottage "Over the Glen" as a deep gorge lined with creeping pine and carpeted with mosses separates it from the dwelling on either side."

Daily Resorter, July 28, 1894

GEORGE STOCKBRIDGE 1888 CRAIGSMERE

George Stockbridge of Kalamazoo, a nephew of Michigan Senator Francis Stockbridge, hired Edwin Zander from his hometown to build his cottage in 1888. Zander was already working on Frank and May Clark's cottage next door. Newspaper descriptions of these early cottages make the point that they were rather small, nondescript dwellings in need of extensive remodeling. That was exactly the step taken by Edward Pitkin of Chicago, Illinois after he purchased of the cottage in 1893. He hired architect Asbury Buckley to remodel it.

Edward Hand Pitkin's glass manufacturing shop led that industry at the time. Starting with $6,000 and a shanty on Chicago's lakeshore, it grew to outfit major hotels and large institutions with his specialty, cut glassware. He married Lillie Elizabeth Morey in 1871.

In 1902, the cottage was sold to Hugh H. Hanna of Indianapolis, Indiana on his retirement from Atlas Engine Works, where he served as president. He also hired the architect Asbury Buckley to remodel in an architectural style that was unusual for the bluffs. What developed according to Buckley's plans was a two-story Classical Revival fronted with a two-story entrance portico flanked with one-story porticos.

By 1919, Craigsmere changed hands again. It passed to Delos and Daisy Blodgett's grown daughters, Helen and Mona. Helen, in a letter to an interested student at the University of Michigan, described the cottage as, "a stucco, Italian style house with a flat roof." The Blodgett sisters and their husbands owned the cottage from 1919 through 1957; however, Mackinac was their summer residence only on alternate years due to their extensive travel.

"F. M. Clark and George Stockbridge of Kalamazoo have leased the lots at National Park next to Pontiac's Lookout and will build early next spring."

Daily Resorter, August 29, 1885

1888 CASSA VERONA
FRANK & MAY CLARK

May (Hoffman) and Frank Miner Clark of Kalamazoo, Michigan leased this lot on the West Bluff in 1886 finally building a small cottage in 1888. Clark had already built a cottage in Gurdon Hubbard's Annex by 1883, one of the first five to build in that development. Around 1893, the Clarks sold the cottage for $8,500.

The new owners, Delos Blodgett's family from Grand Rapids, Michigan, were familiar faces on the Island, having spent many happy summers residing in their other cottage, Isala Bella (see West Bluff Cottage 3). Delos Blodgett, a widow for three years following the death of his wife of thirty-one years, Jennie S. Wood Blodgett, remarried in 1893. His new bride, daughter of Georgia Professor William Henry Peck, was Daisy Peck.

Delos and Daisy had three children: Helen; Delos A., Jr.; and Mona P. Helen, married to Henry Parsons Erwin of Washington, D. C., responded to Mrs. F. G. Hammett, a student at The University of Michigan in 1965, who was writing a seminar paper, "Society Summer Sojourns." The response was a letter describing many aspects of their summers on the Island, particularity how this cottage came into the Blodgett family.

"This place on the corner of one of the roads fronted on a cliff with a magnificent view over the Straits but there was already a small house on it, which discouraged my father. My mother however, asked him to make an offer for it, which he did and in due time a large three-story frame house was built, the smaller one being pushed back to form the kitchen and laundry portions of this house. The house was finished in about 1895 and was typical of the period with several gabled roofs, a large porch running across the front and one side of the house, and at least three second floor balconies. An odd thing is that there was installed a very large window which today would be touted as a picture window, on the side fronting the lake."

Cassa Verona is over one hundred years old. A memorable two-and-a-half story Queen Anne, with a gambrel roof, corner tower, wrap-around porch, stone chimney, and swag friezes, fronts the cliff with a magnificent view of the straits.

"Next Mrs. D. B. Blodgett's beautiful 'summer home' has been translated into the Mexican or Spanish 'Cassa Verona.' Mrs. Blodgett spent last winter in Mexico and there hit upon this musical name."

Daily Resorter, July 28, 1894

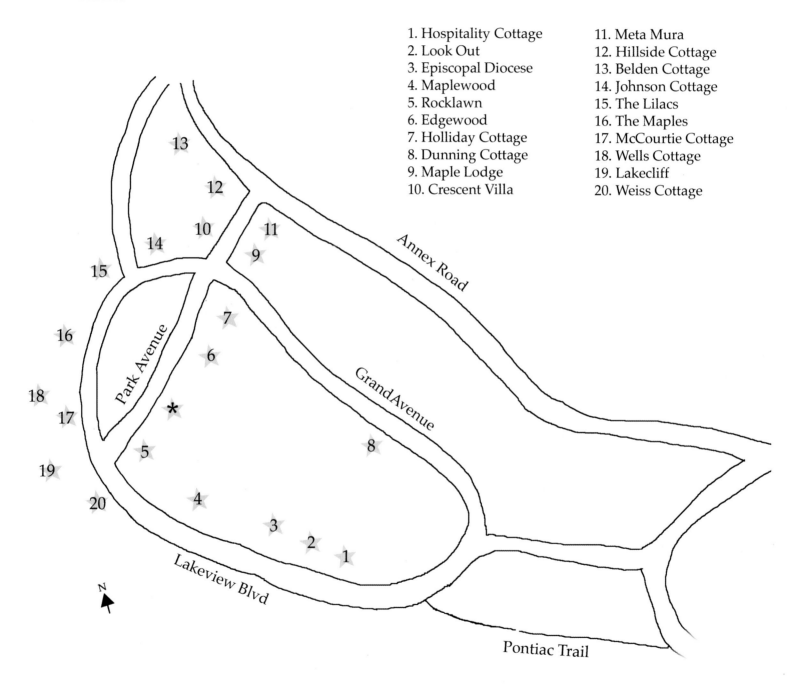

Mackinac Island

Hubbard's Annex

The Cottages

1. Hospitality Cottage
2. Look Out
3. Episcopal Diocese
4. Maplewood
5. Rocklawn
6. Edgewood
7. Holliday Cottage
8. Dunning Cottage
9. Maple Lodge
10. Crescent Villa
11. Meta Mura
12. Hillside Cottage
13. Belden Cottage
14. Johnson Cottage
15. The Lilacs
16. The Maples
17. McCourtie Cottage
18. Wells Cottage
19. Lakecliff
20. Weiss Cottage

Annex Road

Grand Avenue

Park Avenue

Lakeview Blvd

Pontiac Trail

N

HUBBARD'S ANNEX

"The ideal resort of the north may be found at Mackinac in what is known as the 'Annex,' situated on the bluff in the immediate vicinity of 'Lover's Leap' and 'Pontiac's Lookout.' It consists of a plat of ground on which are built some of the prettiest and most elegant cottages in Northern Michigan, owned and occupied by people whose refined and artistic taste, make the spot wonderfully attractive. All who are fortunate enough to reside at this spot enjoy the cool breezes that sweep across the straits. All the cottagers take their meals in a large club house, the Wak-Cheo, this doing away with kitchens at their homes and reaping the advantages of the excellent catering of the steward, John A. Baker, who has had valuable experience at the Peninsular Club in Grand Rapids, and is able to set a most delicious table. There is [sic] about fifteen cottages built on spacious lots covered with beautiful trees, and romantic paths lead to all parts of the Island."

Daily Resorter, August 16, 1887

      Hubbard's Annex includes twenty residences ranging from quaint Carpenter Gothic cottages to stately Colonial Revival mansions. In contrast to the privately owned structures on leased state park land on the East and West Bluffs, the Annex is private land. The neighborhood name was given by Chicago pioneer Gurdon S. Hubbard, who platted the old Davenport Farm into lots. It is officially known on plat maps as Hubbard's Annex to the National Park. Mackinac Island *National* Park existed from 1875 until 1895 when it became a *state* park. The tour begins at the western end of the West Bluff and circles a small park counter-clockwise.

HUGH AND EMMA MCCURDY HOSPITALITY COTTAGE
1885 - 1886

Emma J. and Hugh McCurdy had this cottage built in 1885-1886 when he was a prominent Mason and a successful fifty-six year old lawyer from Corunna, Michigan. Hubbard's Annex to the Mackinac Island National Park was well established, with fourteen cottages and a community Eating House already erected. Gurdon Hubbard, a Chicago pioneer, built the first cottage in 1870, then developed the resort community in 1882.

McCurdy was born in Hamilton, Scotland in 1829, then migrated with his family to Birmingham, Michigan when he was eight years old. Michigan became a state that same year, 1837. He had no formal education until after he became an apprentice cooper in his early teens. Cooperage was a well-respected occupation for a young Scottish lad, wooden barrels being the primary container for shipping anything in the mid-nineteenth century. J. R. Corson and Dr. E. Raynale recognized McCurdy's potential and inspired him to begin his education. While working as a freight agent for the Detroit & Pontiac Railroad, McCurdy began to study law.

"Judge Hugh McCurdy of Corunna, Mich., has been enjoying all the comforts of home at the cottage the 'Hospitaler' [sic] for the past month. Mr. McCurdy is the Past Grand Master of the Knights Templar, and one of the most prominent Masons in the country."

Daily Resorter, July 1901

McCurdy was only eighteen when he took over the classroom, teaching at the village schools, first in Birmingham, then Royal Oak, before furthering his own education at the Romeo Academy. After studying and working for the Pontiac law firm, Baldwin & Draper, McCurdy was admitted to the Michigan bar in 1854 at the age of twenty-five. He moved to Corunna, Michigan, northeast of the new state capital at Lansing, to practice. In Corunna, McCurdy served as prosecutor, probate judge, and state senator. He established the First National Bank of Corunna and served as its president for eight years.

McCurdy was initiated as a Free and Accepted Mason in 1850 when he was twenty-one. His involvement as a Mason was extensive throughout his life. On October 2, 1873, as Grand Master of the Grand Lodge of Michigan, McCurdy had the honor of laying the cornerstone of the new Capitol Building. It was "erected at the bidding of a young but generous commonwealth, and which shall rival in magnitude and grandeur, many an Eastern temple, that told its silent story to whispering winds, four thousand years ago," he proclaimed in the dedication ceremony. Fourteen years later, McCurdy would be called upon again, this time to dedicate the guest register at the grand opening of the Grand Hotel on Mackinac Island on July 10, 1887.

Before the dedication of the Grand, the McCurdys had already built his turreted clapboard Queen Anne summer house with a sweeping, curved veranda. Window details abound in the McCurdy cottage. The front gable features matching roundels flanking paired centered double-hung casement windows. Centered in the front gable is a Palladian window. Yet another oval window fills the span between the gable and the three-story turret. Imbricated shingles cover the conical roof turret. The detail on the second-floor turret windows resembles a Gothic sash. Barred, half-circle ventilation openings line the base of the porch, while multi-paned windows complete the interesting appearance of the cottage.

Masonic business called McCurdy away from his Island home the summer of 1892, when he traveled to Denver, Colorado. There the members elected him most eminent grand master of the grand encampment of Knights Templar for the United States of America, to serve for three years in this position.

The cottage remained in the McCurdy family until after Hugh McCurdy died. A memorial to him is Hugh McCurdy Park in Corunna, Michigan. This thirty-acre recreational area is the home of the Corunna Historical Village of Shiawassee County.

2 LOOK OUT 1893

HOWARD and ABBIE LONGYEAR

The Longyears and the Douglases co-owned this cottage but did not spend the entire summer here, even the first summer in 1893. Dr. Howard Longyear and Samuel T. Douglas of Detroit were both founding members of the exclusive Huron Mountain Club in remote Marquette County, Michigan. Longyear is said to have spent a part of every summer there from the time he helped to found the Club in 1889 until his death in 1921.

Longyear was born in Lansing in 1852. His father, J. W. Longyear, was an attorney and became United States District Court Judge at Detroit. Howard Longyear's older brother, John, found his success in the Upper Peninsula in timber and iron mines. Howard Longyear finished medical school in 1875 and studied in Berlin, Vienna, and Birmingham, England before returning to Michigan. He became the medical superintendent of Harper Hospital in Detroit. Longyear had given up his general practice to specialize in gynecology and abdominal surgery before building the cottage.

Howard Longyear married Abbie Scott of Chicago in 1880, daughter of eminent lawyer, Ira Scott. They had two daughters, Esther and Margaret, who undoubtedly played on the bluff in front of the cottage overlooking the Straits of Mackinac. Perhaps it was the magic of

Mackinac or Longyear's love for the Huron Mountains that caused him to seek more freedom in summer. By 1895, he switched from administration to teaching, becoming the Chair of Clinical Gynecology at the Detroit College of Medicine. He remained a consulting physician at three hospitals and wrote journal articles and an authoritative gynecological monograph. This career move freed him to pursue another business venture with his brother John, the Universal Fastening & Button Company. This business manufactured two-prong fasteners used for attaching shoe buttons fashionable in those days. They later won gold medals at the Louisiana Purchase Exposition in St. Louis in 1904 and at the San Francisco World's Fair in 1915 for their fully automatic shoe button attaching machines.

In addition to his financial success, brother John Longyear is known in Marquette, Michigan as having built a lovely stone mansion on the lakeshore there, but then in 1908, moving it stone by stone to Brookline, Massachusetts where it stands to this day.

The co-owners of the cottage, Samuel T. and Marion Dwight Douglas had only been married two years when the cottage was built. Mr. Douglas was born in Ann Arbor in 1853. His father, Dr. Silas H. Douglas, was a pioneer chemistry pro-

fessor at The University of Michigan. Samuel's uncle, after whom he was named, was a revered attorney, known as "The father of the Detroit Bar," (The *Detroit News*, May 11, 1890). Douglas joined his uncle's law firm upon his admission to the bar and was distinguished as a corporation attorney. Samuel and Marion Douglas had a daughter and a son.

Records indicate that Charles W. Caskey, builder of the Grand Hotel, also built the Longyear cottage; however, boards uncovered during remodeling of the cottage revealed the name of another builder, Patrick Doud. This cottage is a simple Caskey design, a small, symmetrical, cross-gabled vernacular cottage. It has undergone extensive changes to the exterior. A sun porch with multi-paned windows on the east flanks a three-sided bay window with a screen porch on the west.

The Longyears did not remain Mackinac cottagers for long. After the 1897 season, they sold their interest to Marion Douglas. In April 1900, J.P. Cunningham inquired about renting the "Douglas cottage." Mackinac Island State Park Superintendent Samuel Poole replied that the Douglas cottage was indeed a desirable location. The *Daily Resorter* reported in July 1901 that, "Mrs. H. de Jonge of Detroit is occupying the Douglas cottage this season." In 1906, the Douglases sold the cottage to Alastair and Isabella Valentine of Chicago.

"Just west of Mr. McCurdy's, Dr. Longyear and S. T. Douglas of Detroit have built a beautiful cottage and christened it 'Look Out.'"

Daily Resorter, July 17, 1893

EPISCOPAL DIOCESE
1885

This cottage has its origin in the religious life of Mackinac Island. The Episcopal Church is one of three Protestant denominations with a history on the Island. The Reverend William Ferry laid the cornerstone of Mission Church in 1829. Mission Church had its roots in a Presbyterian congregation Ferry organized in 1823. Little Stone Church is a Congregational church, built in 1904. In 1882, Trinity Episcopal Church was built below the Fort using soldiers' donations and pledges. St. Anne's Roman Catholic Church dates back to 1780 on the Island itself and even earlier at Fort Michilimackinac. When the British relocated the Fort from the mainland to the Island, they hauled the church building across the ice.

By 1885 when this cottage was built, the Episcopal Church was well established on Mackinac Island. The Episcopal Diocese of Michigan built it here in Hubbard's Annex to the Mackinac Island National Park to serve as its bishop's summer cottage. Hubbard's Annex was well established and into its third season as a resort community. Eleven cottages and a community Eating House were already erected, and two other cottages were under construction, but the future site of the Grand Hotel was still a vacant lot. The first bishop to enjoy the cottage was Rev. Samuel Smith Harris.

credit Mackinac State Historic Parks, Michigan

Rev. Harris traveled a road to church leadership different from others. He was born in 1841 to wealthy Southern planters. At age eighteen, he was the youngest person the University of Alabama had graduated; then after he studied law briefly, it required a special act of the legislature to admit him to the bar at his young age. He barely had time to start a practice in Montgomery, Alabama when the Civil War broke out. During the war, he married Mary Pickett, also from a Southern planter family, and reached the rank of lieutenant colonel in the Confederate Army. The years of war did not slow him down. By 1865 at only age twenty-four, he was practicing law in New York City. His practice specialized in cases before the Supreme Court of New York. In the years he practiced there, he never lost a Supreme Court case.

As successful as Harris was as an attorney, his heart called him in a different direction. At age twenty-eight, he switched careers, studying theology to become an Episcopal priest. He returned to the turbulent South still in the Reconstruction period moving north later in 1875 to become the rector at St. James Church in Chicago. In 1879, at age thirty-eight, he was elected the second bishop of the Michigan diocese. Six years into the job, with over thirty-five churches and chapels built and with a church congregation established in forty other locations throughout Michigan, The Diocese purchased a lot in Hubbard's Annex on July 3, 1885. The grateful church members built this cottage for Rev. Harris and his family.

Rev. Harris was only forty-seven when he died July 3, 1888, in England. He had but two seasons to enjoy this cottage on Mackinac, overlooking the straits. Bishop Harris' son, Samuel S. Harris, returned to the Island over the years, at times staying with cottager friends such as T. Stewart White on the West Bluff (see West Bluff cottage 11). The younger Harris graduated from The University of Michigan and became a prominent lawyer in Detroit.

The Rev. Thomas F. Davies succeeded Harris as Bishop. With his wife and daughter Marion, the Davies family summered at the Diocese cottage for many years.

This simple Caskey-designed cottage has undergone very little change to the exterior. It remains a small, symmetrical, cross-gabled vernacular cottage decorated with applied Carpenter Gothic ornamentation. Turned porch posts and scroll sawn brackets support the wraparound veranda. Scroll sawn brackets support the front gable, and saw-tooth shingles clad its peak.

MAPLEWOOD

HENRY & NIANA DAVIS 1894

"Col. Henry Davis, Jr. of Springfield, Illinois broke ground today for a new cottage next to Bishop Davies' summer home. The work on the building will be pushed and the cottage will be enclosed before fall, making it possible to finish the inside in time for next season. A. W. Buckley, who is known as the architect of most of the cottages on the Island will design and superintend the building of this one for Col. Davis and says that it will be equal in every way to the best cottage on the Island. Col. Davis was delayed in building this summer on account of the strike at Chicago, he being called there in command of the Illinois National Guard. "

Daily Resorter, August 8, 1894

The Davis cottage is one of the few in Hubbard's Annex not built by contactor Charles W. Caskey, partly because it was built after the Caskey building boom in the mid-1880s. In 1891, with more of his work off the Island, Caskey sold his personal Annex home and moved to Petoskey. The year before this cottage was built, Mr. Caskey did build the neighboring cottage for Longyear and Douglas (see Annex Cottage 2), but in most respects, he was no longer a Mackinac Island builder.

Instead, Colonel Henry and Niana Davis of Springfield, Illinois hired Asbury W. Buckley. Buckley was an architect, but for the Davis project, he served as general contractor, too. Buckley worked primarily on the West Bluff, but built this cottage, his sole construction project in the Annex. He was not involved in another Mackinac Island project until eight years later when he remodeled the West Bluff cottage for H. H. Hanna, the same cottage he remodeled in 1893 for Edward Pitkin (see West

Bluff Cottage 12). The Davises paid $10,000 for their new cottage.

This style, new to the Annex in 1894, is Colonial Revival. A prominent characteristic of this style is a hipped roof, here topped with a widow's walk sur-

rounded by an iron railing. A front gable clad with imbricated shingles and a Palladian window, projects from the south slope of the roof and is the focal point of the symmetrical mass of the structure. Similar gables project from other sides of the cottage. Symmetrical three-sided bay windows with multi-paned glass frame

the front gable. Double columns, now with one end enclosed with multi-paned windows, support the porch. Saw tooth shingles enclose the area under the porch vented through lattice grillwork. The house rises two-and-one-half stories on a raised foundation.

Colonel Davis, a distinguished-appearing man, was a banker and owned a substantial amount of farmland in the Springfield, lllinois area. From Illinois they brought two horses, a cow, and chickens. Mrs. Davis was much younger than the Colonel, and they were known for their social life. They frequently entertained other cottagers: the Bruckners, the Herts, the McArthurs, the Puttkammers, the Days, the Cudahys, and the Blodgetts. Colonel Davis passed away at his Annex home.

FRANK ᵃⁿᵈ MAY CLARK
ROCKLAWN

1883, 1900

This cottage is one of two that Frank and May Clark built on the Island. Rocklawn was built first in 1883, while the other was built five years later on West Bluff (see West Bluff Cottage 13). The Clarks were among the first families to build a cottage in Gurdon Hubbard's Annex to the National Park. At this time East and West Bluffs were empty, cedar-covered bluffs. The Grand Hotel was still a dream of Francis Stockbridge. The National Park lagged behind demand in issuing leases for building lots. Hubbard's private lots met the market demand.

Gurdon Hubbard, who had been enjoying his summer home here since 1870, was now seventy years old and nearly blind, but he had the vision of a resort community tucked away on his quiet tract of land. He recruited eight other families to join The Mackinac Island Resort Association and to share their meals at a communal Eating House. Five of these families were from Kalamazoo, Michigan. Frank Clark, along with Hezekiah Wells, William McCourtie, Theodore Sheldon, and Francis Stockbridge formed the Wacheo Club and built their cottages around a park in Hubbard's Annex.

Frank M. Clark was born in 1842 in New York, but had come to

Kalamazoo at an early age with his parents. His father established a general store there, but it later became an exclusive dry goods store known for silks, laces, and linens. Clark took over the store when his father died and managed it until 1894. He was also a director of the First National Bank and a member of the board of directors of Bardeen Paper Company.

Thirty-one-year old Clark and Miss May Hoffman of New York City were married in 1873. They had one daughter, Grace Eleanor, and had been married for ten years when they built this cottage.

The cottage they first built is buried within this structure. It was a simple cross-gabled two-story Carpenter Gothic built by Charles Caskey. In the projecting front (west) gable of the house, one distinguishing feature of the original house is still apparent, the north entry door. The north-facing gable, hidden from street view by an addition, displays the original bargeboard with a drop pendant. In 1883, cast iron ridge cresting, turned wood porch rails and posts, lattice screening, scroll sawn sunburst pendants, and a row of decorative medallions ornamented the cottage.

In 1888, after thinking about it for

The Clarks' 1883 Annex cottage and 1888 West Bluff cottage show striking similarities, credit Rosalie Roush collection.

Rocklawn after 1900 remodeling, credit Rosalie Roush collection

"In what is known as the Annex is the delightful summer residence of Mr. Frank M. Clark of Kalamazoo which is facetiously named by its genial owner 'Rocklawn' because says he, 'it is a continued struggle between rocks and lawn to see which will beat.'"

Daily Resorter, July 28, 1894

years and forfeiting one lease, the Clarks built a West Bluff cottage on the leased National Park lot closest to their Annex cottage. Hammers were ringing as nine of the sixteen West Bluff cottages were built that year. The Clarks maintained both cottages for five years.

In 1893, May died and Clark sold the West Bluff cottage to Delos and Daisy Blodgett. Frank Clark retreated to the original Annex cottage. The following year, he sold the dry goods store, and retired at age fifty-two.

Throughout the late 1890s, Clark was instrumental in improving water sources to the Annex and West Bluff cottagers. With David Hogg from the West Bluff, Clark organized the cottagers to lay a small pipe and install a series of pumps to bring water up the bluff from the lake. Previously the cottagers had Mike Norwijagig, an Island Anishinabe leader, deliver drinking water by dray from the spring below the fort. They used rainwater cisterns for other water needs. In 1900 and 1901, Clark provided water to Justice William Day who regularly rented a cottage across the commons (see Annex Cottage 16). In 1901, a municipal water system was installed on the Island.

Keeping up with the other cottagers, Clark remodeled Rocklawn in 1900. This was only one of many successive projects. A third floor was added, as were more rooms on the second floor. A large two-story addition was built on the back of the house, the porches were expanded, and the entry stairs were reconfigured. It is likely that a kitchen was added when the communal Eating House discontinued service.

At age seventy, Clark married a second time, to Mrs. Maude Mason Ranney in Paris, France. They traveled extensively in Europe and the U.S., collecting paintings, book prints, bric-a-brac, and carved furniture. They were married seven years before he died in Kalamazoo in May 1919. According to his obituary, Clark still "maintained a summer residence on Mackinac Island, where he went early in June and remained until late in the season."

After the 1926 summer season, Mrs. Clark sold the cottage to Luther and Ida Day. Luther Day was one of the four sons of U. S. Supreme Court Justice William R. Day of Ohio. The William R. Day family had rented a cottage across the commons for many years from the time Luther was a young boy. Luther Day, born in 1879, married Ida McKinley Barber in 1903 while he was a law student at The University of Michigan. Ida Day was the niece of U. S. President William McKinley. Luther and Ida Day had two daughters, Ida and Katherine. Mr. Day practiced law for fifty-three years in northeastern Ohio as a trial and corporation attorney. According to his February 8, 1965 *Cleveland Press* obituary, "'Lute', as he was known to his friends, backed up his opinions with logic that rolled forth in oratory that held courtroom attendants spellbound."

6 1883 THEODORE SHELDON EDGEWOOD

Theodore Sheldon was the first to own this cottage built in 1883 by Charles W. Caskey, later the builder of the Grand Hotel. Sheldon belonged to The Mackinac Island Resort Association. The five of the original nine Association families from Kalamazoo, Michigan—Frank Clark, Hezekiah Wells, William McCourtie, Theodore Sheldon, and Francis Stockbridge—formed the Wacheo Club, and they built their cottages around the park in Hubbard's Annex close to the communal Eating House. Sheldon's cottage was most convenient to the Eating House located just to the south. Sheldon served as treasurer of the Resort Association.

Sheldon's wealth came from the private bank that he established in 1844. Within twenty years, during the Civil War, he had the highest annual income of any man in Kalamazoo. This is evident from the records kept of taxes to raise funds for the war that Kalamazoo imposed on incomes of more than $600. Sheldon's income was shown to be $8,850, including $1,000 of interest on U. S. government bonds.

Mrs. Sheldon served as president of the Kalamazoo Ladies' Aid Society in 1863. The women raised more than $5,000 for blankets and hospital supplies and for the relief of wounded soldiers and their families. The next year the Society organized a State Sanitary Fair, raising $9,300.

The original 1883 cottage can still be seen; however, there have been some modifications. Over the years, owners have added a sun porch to the south side of the house and enclosed the south end of the porch. A pitched roof dormer once over the window south of the front door has been exchanged for a similar dormer

projecting from the south side of the main gable.

The entry stairs still run off the porch from the corner at an angle, but they are not as wide and comply with modern building codes that require handrails. Some new Carpenter Gothic ornamentation has been reapplied, particularly at the front gable peak, but neither the original finial nor the ridge cresting has been re-applied. Turned posts replaced the scroll sawn railings on the lower porch and on the sun porch roof.

Like the other cottages in Hubbard's Annex, this lovely structure is private property. Please respect the privacy of the occupants and do not trespass.

credit Mackinac State Historic Parks, Michigan

7 DR. DANIEL HOLLIDAY
HOLLIDAY COTTAGE
1883

Of all the original cottagers, Dr. Daniel Chemiere Holliday, a physician from New Orleans, Louisiana, traveled the farthest to a summer residence on Mackinac Island. Dr. Holliday was born in 1824 in Louisiana. His parents, John Robert and Maria Holliday, appear to have owned Belle Grove Plantation near what later became New Orleans International Airport. When Daniel was only eight years old, his father died, then his mother died when he was eighteen and in school at the College of William and Mary. This did not stop the young man. Holliday continued his education, receiving a medical degree from the University of Pennsylvania. Thereafter, Holliday studied in Europe, then returned to New Orleans to practice medicine. Malaria was a disease of great interest to Dr. Holliday, and he wrote a number of articles on the subject.

By 1850 Dr. Holliday lived with two overseers and a teacher, but no women or children, near the family plantation owned by his older half-sister Eliza Davis Kenner and her husband Minor Kenner. Curiously, records indicate that Dr. Holliday had one daughter, Felicie, born in 1840, when he was sixteen years old. Perhaps she lived separately with her mother or with her Aunt Eliza. His other children, Noemie (or Minnia) and Daniel, were born much later in 1858 and 1869, respectively. Felicie later lived with her father, in 1880 when she was the widow of Arthur Guillotte.

Dr. Holliday was fifty-nine years old when his Mackinac Island cottage was built here in Hubbard's Annex among five other cottages owned by young families from Kalamazoo, Michigan. It was one of nine cottages that Charles W. Caskey built in 1883. Dr. Holliday died in 1889, six years after Caskey built the cottage.

Dr. Frank Billings and his wife Dane Ford Brawley Billings rented this cottage. It is diagonally across the Annex park from the cottage rented by Billings' close friend Dr. Lewis Linn McArthur, also of Chicago. Dr. Billings was a major figure in the Chicago medical scene during the early cottage period.

Billings graduated from the Chicago Medical College (later known as Northwestern University Medical College) in 1881. Billings and McArthur interned together and later shared the same

credit Mackinac State Historic Parks, Michigan

medical offices in Chicago. In addition to his medical practice, Billings taught at Northwestern University Medical College and at the University of Chicago's Rush Medical College where he served as dean of the faculty for twenty years. From 1902 until 1904, Billings was president of the American Medical Association.

Billings' practice brought him into contact with the wealthiest of the wealthy of Chicago: Philip Armour, Marshall Field, George Pullman, the McCormicks, and the Palmers. However, Billings did not neglect to treat the poorest of the poor, and he used his position of influence with the wealthy to solicit donations for charitable and educational medical institutions. For example, because of his friendship with Billings, Orson Welles donated his entire estate to the University of Chicago. Many of McArthur's and Billings' wealthy patients summered at Mackinac Island.

Dane Billings was an accomplished pianist and assisted her husband in running the medical practice. Frank and Dane Billings had one daughter, Marga-

"The family of Dr. Frank Billings are in their cottage for the season. Mr. Billings is expected about the middle of the month."

Daily Resorter, July 1901

ret. Tragically, Mrs. Billings died of Bright's Disease at a young age in 1896. Thereafter, Dr. Billings became both father and mother to his young daughter. With such a busy professional life, father and daughter would have treasured the time they spent together at the cottage in the Annex

"Dr. Billings is expected next week from Chicago and will bring with him Dr. Dickerman who will spend time on the Island."

Daily Resorter, July 11, 1902

away from those demands.

The modern Holliday cottage is one of the best surviving examples of Caskey's simple design. As such, it is a small, symmetrical, cross-gabled vernacular structure with a wrap-around porch, decorated with applied Carpenter's Gothic ornamentation. The eaves of the front gable have been extended to form a porch overhang on the second level. A railing encloses this second-floor porch. The lower wrap-around porch corner was angled off. Wider steps with handrails have replaced the narrower set. Porch posts and rails come and go over time, but the round windows that symmetrically pierce the flank of the cross-gable section remain constant.

Dunning Cottage

William & Anna Dunning 1885 – 1886

Gurdon Hubbard had Charles W. Caskey build a smaller cottage here away from the main commons of the Annex in 1885-86. That original cottage can be seen in the center of the structure. The living room occupied the entire first floor under the front center gable. On the second floor was a sleeping area. The porch wrapped around the structure. In March 1890, Hubbard sold the cottage to William and Anna (Hines) Dunning of Detroit. They wanted a place to get away from the heat of the city for a couple of weeks each summer with their two daughters, Bertha and Clara.

Dunning was a salesman. He traveled extensively selling various things from wholesale groceries to elevators, but insurance seemed to be his most profitable product. Dunning hired a young lawyer, Abraham Lincoln, to collect some accounts in Illinois before Lincoln became preoccupied with politics. On one business trip, Dunning wrote a letter to his wife back in Detroit describing the fires he saw in Indianapolis that the striking railroad union organizers had set.

The Dunnings did not need a large showplace on Mackinac Island, just a cool family retreat. They owned a horse farm in Rochester, Michigan from which they brought some good horses and a groomsman to the little barn.

The Dunnings added the rear lean-to over the years. When the community Eating House closed, they added the kitchen with a maid's room. When water was piped to the Annex, they added a bathroom.

Bertha, or "Birdie," Dunning married Dr. Allan McDonald. They honeymooned on Mackinac Island, a family tradition until 1998 when the Dunning descendents sold the cottage. Dr. McDonald had a successful medical practice in Detroit, but when the Island doctor left for World War II, McDonald sold his practice and moved full time to the Island. Living in this cottage in the warmer weather and moving to an apartment in the Village for the winters, he served the Island residents' medical needs. Dr. McDonald added the hip roofed corner towers.

"Where Grand Avenue runs into the Annex, there is on the left side, a very charming grove of trees, nestled down among which lies the beautiful summer home of W. H. Dunning. Mr. Dunning, accompanied by his wife and two daughters, the Misses Birdie and Clara, have been here for the past month."

Daily Resorter, August 28, 1894

MAPLE LODGE

CHARLES and EDITH CASKEY

"C. W. Caskey's cottage No. 2 is occupied by himself, and family and friends."

Daily Resorter, August 29, 1885

The work of no other hand is as apparent on Mackinac Island as that of Charles W. Caskey, contractor and builder. Living in this cottage built in 1884, Caskey managed the construction of the Island's most visible structure, the Grand Hotel three years later in 1887. Charles W. Caskey, born in Allegan, Michigan in 1850, moved his construction business north in about 1880 to take advantage of the summer cottage building boom. Beginning with a cottage for E. H. Pope in Wequetonsing, Michigan that year, he would build over one thousand cottages, the Petoskey Opera House, and several hotels in the next five years. Caskey also built many cottages in the communities of Harbor Springs, Petoskey, and Bay View. Caskey relocated his family from Allegan to Harbor Springs where he operated a lumberyard as well, and he built a home for them there in 1882.

Caskey's crew completed the carpentry work on his Harbor Springs home in less than one week! This speed of construction was critical in building cottages for short summer seasons and was to become the foundation of Caskey's reputation. He could be so quick because his company controlled the raw materials and the transportation of them to the building sites. He also knew how to organize his workers and keep them on the job.

Caskey was also quick because he built one simple design. His vernacular cottage was a small, symmetrical plan with steeply pitched intersecting gables. The front gable contained the living room paired by windows and surrounded by porch on three sides. Another gable runs perpendicular to the first and contained two rooms, usually the dining room and a bedroom. A single-story lean-to attached to the back provided space for the kitchen and servants. Three bedrooms were typically over the living room, dining room, and first floor bedroom. The exterior appearance was also standard—railed porches, interior chimneys, and applied Carpenter Gothic ornamentation. Owners could choose colors, trims, and the location of windows and porch steps. Finials often topped the high peaks and drop pendants decorated the bargeboards of the eaves.

Caskey built the entire Annex community of 1883. To handle the demand, he set up a lumberyard at St. Ignace, which was closer to the Annex than Harbor Springs. His crews hammered out the communal Eating House. Caskey and his crews built a second cottage for Hubbard next to Hubbard's original thirteen-year-old cottage, as well as completed the cottages of Frank Clark, Theodore Sheldon, Hezekiah Wells, William McCourtie, all of Kalamazoo; of Otis Johnson of Racine, Wisconsin; and of Daniel Holliday from New Orleans, Louisiana.

The 1883 Mackinac construction season was so successful for Caskey that he personally bought several lots from Hubbard in August. It is likely that Caskey built the summer palace of Francis Stockbridge and another cottage for attorney Edwin Street (later torn down), both from Kalamazoo, in the Annex over the winter. On the land he bought from Hubbard, he built this cottage for his own

credit Lorna Straus Collection

family in 1884 and two rental units across the street in 1885. One of the rental houses sold the first season, while the other was rented for years by a family who later bought it.

Caskey varied his standard design in this cottage for his own personal use. Maple Lodge is larger and more elaborate than his usual vernacular design. The most noticeable difference is the tower with a concave mansard roof, rising four stories from the ground with a shed dormer window on each side. This tower was removed when the third floor and roof top deck were added. Still visible are remnants of the two original front gables with the old tower reduced to a third gable.

Caskey's popularity as the Mackinac Island cottage builder did not wane in 1885. His services were hired on the East Bluff to build the cottages of Phebe Gehr (see East Bluff Cottage 11) and Charlotte Warren (see East Bluff Cottage 12), both from Chicago. The Episcopal Diocese of Michigan also contracted with Caskey to build its bishop a summer residence in the Annex just down the block and around the corner from Caskey's own (see Annex Cottage 3).

Caskey was the logical choice as the builder of the Grand Hotel. The thirty-seven-year-old contractor had the crews, the equipment, the materials, the skills, and the reputation to build a one thousand-guest hotel with a six hundred-foot long front porch in time for the 1887 summer season. George Mason of the Detroit firm of Mason & Rice prepared the plans. Caskey and three hundred workers built the Grand in less than four months, using 1.5 million feet of lumber, and hauling supplies from the mainland across the ice late in the winter. The Hotel opened on sched-ule on July 10, 1887.

Building the Grand is said to have made Caskey a wealthy man just seven years after he moved north. Perhaps he no longer needed the money from as many projects after the Grand or maybe it was just time to relax a bit. In any event, he is known to have built only one cottage in each of the next two years. In 1888, he built the G. W. Smith cottage (see East Bluff

Cottage 10), then in 1889, the Gilbert cottage (see West Bluff Cottage 8). In 1891, Caskey built a cottage for E. P. Barnard (see East Bluff Cottage 6) and sold Maple Lodge. Because he was without a summer home base on the Island or possibly due to the depression of 1893, Caskey built only one more cottage on the Island, the Look Out for Longyear and Douglas (see Annex Cottage 2). The Caskey family invested in the growth of Petoskey with a planing mill and a furniture factory. In 1895, he built and thereafter managed the unsuccessful Imperial Hotel there, constucted around his own large home. It burned in 1908. With two sons and a daughter, Caskey moved to Seattle, Washington where he continued building houses. He died in 1933 in Washington.

Another distinguished early resident of Maple Lodge was Dr. Lewis Linn McArthur, a physician from Chicago. Dr. McArthur rented one of Caskey's houses across the street to the west for many years, bought it, and then traded cottages with the second owner of Maple Lodge in 1897.

10

1885
CRESCENT VILLA

DR LEWIS AND MAMIE MCARTHUR

Charles W. Caskey built this cottage as a rental unit in 1885. He repeated his typical cross-gabled design with a wrap-around front porch and applied Carpenter Gothic ornamentation. A variation here is the jerkinhead or clipped gable on the front façade. The south end of the porch has been enclosed and another sunroom constructed on the second floor above the enclosure. The bracketed second-story balcony remains the same as does the scroll sawn spandrels, brackets, cornice trim, and porch railing. The star pattern has been carefully preserved. The gabled overhang extending from the porch roof toward the angled front steps is another unusual feature.

Caskey finally sold this cottage in 1890 to regular summer tenants Lewis and Mamie (Walker) McArthur. Dr. McArthur was already a distinguished Chicago physician when the young married couple started renting the cottage from Caskey. McArthur would serve as chief surgeon at St. Luke's Hospital in Chicago for forty-eight years, from 1886 until his death in 1934. Dr. McArthur was considered a leader in the introduction of aseptic surgery.

One of Dr. McArthur's closest friends was Frank Billings. The two doctors interned together at the old Cook County Hospital, shared the same medical offices, and vacationed on Mackinac Island together. Dr. Billings and his family regularly rented the Holliday cottage diagonally across the commons. Mamie and Lewis McArthur even named one of their sons Billings McArthur in honor of their friend. Lewis Linn, Jr. and Selim were the other two sons who spent their childhood summers playing here. Dr. Billings described Dr. McArthur as a "surgeon of surpassing skill and a man with a heart overflowing with kindness and sympathy," when he endowed the McArthur lectureship at the

credit Mackinac State Historic Parks, Michigan

Institute of Medicine of Chicago.

Ernst Puttkammer, another friend from Chicago, came to Mackinac at McArthur's suggestion. Ernst and Meta Puttkammer and their baby boy Ernst Wilfred were patients of Dr. McArthur. He advised them to get their son out of the city and up to Mackinac in the summer for the sake of the child's health. The Puttkammers rented The Lilacs (see Annex Cottage 15) from Mrs. Hubbard, bought a lot, and watched the construction of their own cottage across the street. The Puttkammer cottage came to be owned by the same family longer than any other on Mackinac.

Golf became one of Dr. McArthur's favorite pastimes on the Island. With several others, he set up a six-hole course in the cow pasture west of the Annex. They wanted a real golf course, however. Dr. McArthur, along with John Amberg, another Chicagoan (see West Bluff Cottage 7), negotiated a lease for open land with farmer Peter Early. They called in golf pro Alex Smith, who had just arrived in the States from Scotland, to lay out what became Wawashkamo Golf Club. It was McArthur who signed the construction agreement with contractor Frank Rounds on October 31, 1898 to build the course. McArthur served a president of the Wawashkamo Golf Club in its early years and for later terms as well. He likely gave the club its name from the Indian words for "crooked trail" that he learned from Island Anishinabe leader Mike Norwijagig. *Golf Digest* magazine has designated Wawashkamo as one of nine Historic

"Rev. [sic] L. L. McArthur of Chicago calls his pretty cottage "Crescent Villa" as it stands just on the edge of a crescent-shaped plot, bordering the road."

Daily Resorter, July 28, 1894

Golf Landmarks in America.

With three growing boys and many summer visitors, the McArthurs needed a larger cottage. The Curtis family in the old Caskey residence (see Annex Cottage 9) was ready to downsize. In March 1897, they switched cottages. The McArthurs paid the Curtises $2,750. The Curtises paid the McArthurs $1,250. In about 1917, Selim McArthur hired Patrick Doud to build a cottage secluded in the woods east of the new McArthur cottage. Selim McArthur's cottage was the first modern ranch-style built on the Island.

META MURA
ERNST and META PUTTKAMMER
1894

Dr. Lewis Linn McArthur of Annex Cottage 10 had a hand in this cottage, as well as at least three others. The Puttkammers first came to Mackinac at McArthur's suggestion. Ernst and Meta Puttkammer and their baby boy Wilfred were patients of Dr. McArthur. The baby "was not having a very good first year," as Wilfred later described the situation. Kind Dr. McArthur advised the Puttkammers to get their son out of the city heat and up to Mackinac in the summer for the sake of the child's health. The Puttkammers rented The Lilacs (see Annex Cottage 15) for three seasons, bought land, and watched the construction of their own cottage across the street. Completed for the 1894 season, the Puttkammer cottage, Meta Mura, came to be owned by the same family longer than any other on Mackinac. Dr. McArthur's advice must have been correct for the baby Wilfred

summered on Mackinac until he died at age eighty-seven. At the time of his death, Wilfred was still so vigorous that he was traveling the world aboard a Norwegian vessel in the Indian Ocean bound for Bombay.

The Puttkammers traveled to Europe frequently because that was Ernst's family home. He was born in 1863 in eastern Germany, the oldest son in a family of nobility. Young Ernst Puttkammer, however, had other ideas about his future than to shoulder the responsibilities of managing an estate. He took the second ship out of the closest port (his mother convinced him not to hurry away on the first ship that they later learned sank on its journey!) and docked in New York City. He proceeded to Chicago, and as his finances were depleted, took a position sweeping floors in a coal yard. Before long Puttkammer owned The Edgemont Coal Company, then bought and sold coal mines. Coal being a winter product, Puttkammer had more free time to summer on Mackinac than other businessmen.

Still, Puttkammer did need to leave the family on the Island and return to the business world for periods during the summer. Dr. McArthur had patients to see in Chicago, too. Af-

left: A line drawing of the original Meta Mura, 1894
credit Cordie Puttkammer collection.

ter the McArthurs moved across the road to the old Caskey residence, the family set up a dry cell telephone between the two houses so that the wives could contact each other quickly in case of an emergency. This is likely the first telephone on the Island.

Wilfred was an only child, but summers on the Island were not lonely. In his reminiscences he recalled playing with other Annex children, like Edwin Hennessy, whose family owned the famous cognac company. Puttkammer befriended Henry Faurot, who came with his grandparents, David and Fannie Silverthorne. Of course, he played with the McArthur boys, Lewis, Selim, and Billings. It was a little boy's paradise.

The original cottage that local builder Patrick Doud built for Meta and Ernst Puttkammer was a small two-bedroom one-story bungalow. They did not need much more room since the size of their immediate family was only three people. The Puttkammers expanded the cottage over the years as the family grew and more visitors arrived. They added a second floor, porches, sunrooms, and very important, indoor bathrooms! The cottage evolved with a style of its own, having little in common with the surrounding Caskey cottages except a cross-gable. The Latin word for "walls" was used to convey the meaning "Meta's House," with the musical name "Meta Mura," literally translated "Walls of Meta."

HILLSIDE COTTAGE

12 · ALBERT & CLARA SILVERTHORNE · 1893

When Albert David and Clara "Fannie" Silverthorne built their cottage on the hillside northwest of the Annex commons in 1893, only two of their six living children were unmarried. George was sixteen and Frank was fourteen when they moved into the new cottage.

David's family moved to Iowa from Pennsylvania in a covered wagon when he was three years old. They were one of the first families who settled in that area. David owned a large farm of his own in Pleasant Prairie near his parents' farm and married nineteen-year-old Fannie Hodgekins when he was twenty-six in 1862. Fannie was from Maine where the Hodgekins family was in the lumber business. The business would grow to include operations in not only Maine, but also in the southeastern and the northern states as well. David kept his farm, but he also joined his wife's family in business. With three young sons and a newborn baby daughter, the Silverthornes moved to Chicago just after the Great Fire in 1871. George was born in Chicago, but the youngest, Frank, was born during a visit to the farm. Perhaps the family's farming heritage inspired the cottage's upright and wing plan used in many farmhouses.

The only daughter of David and Fannie, Abby, better known as Catherine, married Henry Faurot. Faurot became part of the Silverthorne lumber business, but he was also involved with Philip D. Armour in a feltworks. When the feltworks burned down, Faurot got Armour's permission to take the employees and, with his lumber profits, start a new company of his own called Western Felt. The company manufactured felt products like horse blankets, billiard table covers, and later, felt products used in the automotive industry. In 1899 young George and his older brother William became associated with Faurot's Western Felt Works.

George still had time to make the trip to Mackinac Island, however, where his arrival on the *Manitou* was announced in the *Daily Resorter*, July 27, 1901. Catherine Silverthorne Faurot may have still been at the cottage. The *Resorter* took note of her presence at the Silverthorne cottage earlier on July 9. It is likely that David and Fannie's grandson, little Henry Faurot, Jr. was along with his mother, playing with ten-year-old Wilfred Puttkammer across the road.

George Silverthorne became vice president of Western Felt before his marriage in 1903 to Edith Hellyer. Edith had been born in Kobe, Japan where her family was in the tea business. George kept the cottage until 1933.

"A. D. Silverthorne, wife, and two sons, Frank and George, both of the Orchard Lake military academy, are fast getting settled for the season in 'Hillside' cottage."

Daily Resorter, July 23, 1894

BELDEN COTTAGE

JOHN & AMANDA BELDEN 1885

Contractor Charles W. Caskey's 1883 building season was so successful that he bought several lots from Gurdon Hubbard for his own speculation. He had built all of the cottages around the Annex commons that year, except of course, for Hubbard's own 1870 cottage The Lilacs. After he built a cottage for his own family on the land across the street, he built this rental house and another just to the south. This cottage is a miniature of Caskey's standard house plan; it is a one-and-a-half story structure rather than two full stories. The intersecting gables are there as well as the applied wood ornamentation. One end and side of the front porch has been enclosed, as well as the opposite side porch.

Caskey rented the cottage for the first season to George Stockbridge, the nephew of Francis Stockbridge. George Stockbridge would have Kalamazoo contractor Edwin Zander build him a cottage on the West Bluff in 1888 (see West Bluff Cottage 13). By the end of the season, however, Caskey sold this little gem to John and Amanda Belden of Chicago for $1,020.00.

John Belden had been in the fire insurance business in Chicago since 1865, before the Great Fire of 1871. He may have known Gurdon Hubbard from his line of business. The Great Fire had been a financial disaster for Hubbard, hence, he was developing the Annex for cash. Belden was a representative of leading American and British insurance companies. He was also a director and the treasurer of the Rialto Company and a director of Belden Manufacturing Company that made insulated wire.

John and Amanda Belden had been married nearly twenty years when they bought the cottage. They had four children: Charles; John, Jr.; Joseph; and Elizabeth. Amanda Belden was from Kalamazoo and probably knew many other Kalamazoo families in the Annex.

credit Mackinac State Historic Parks, Michigan

1883 JOHNSON COTTAGE OTIS and EMILY JOHNSON

14

Otis R. Johnson and his sons, Otis W. and Charles Russell, of Racine, Wisconsin were business associates of Francis Stockbridge (see Annex Cottage 19). Stockbridge and the Johnsons had been trying to build summer cottages on Mackinac Island since the Mackinac Island National Park was created in 1875. The "management plan" for the new national park specified that lots to build private cottages would be surveyed and leased to people of high standing. The income from these leases would fund the park's budget. Two of the first three requests for leases were from Otis W. Johnson and Stockbridge in November 1875. No action was taken on the requests, however, and the means to even survey the park land were not found until nine years later, well after Gurdon Hubbard offered lots for sale in the Annex.

The Johnsons joined the Wacheo Club of Annex cottagers from Kalamazoo and Dr. Holliday from New Orleans, building this cottage on the Annex park in 1883. The original cottage Caskey built can be seen behind the glass-enclosed porches that are topped with a decorative scroll sawn railing. From the side, the structure appears to be two cross-gabled Caskey homes linked by these multi-paned glass-enclosed porches. Carpenter Gothic orna-mentation continues to decorate the barge-boards. The "fine barn" Mr. Bulkley built remains a "fine barn."

The cottage ownership changed hands several times in its early years, from Otis Johnson to William F. and Abby A. Bulkley in 1885, to Peter Hennessey in 1900. Hennessey remains a well-known brand of cognac, but the business and the family suffered during Prohibition. Indeed, in 1919, widower Hennessey put the cottage up for sale. Neighbor Ernst Puttkammer found the buyer.

The Puttkammers of Chicago completed their Annex cottage in 1894 (see Annex Cottage 11). Puttkammer invited his banker William T. Bruckner from the Continental Illinois Bank, to visit his cottage while on a Great Lakes cruise with his wife, Edith. When the Bruckners docked at Mackinac Island, Puttkammer pointed out the Hennessey cottage for sale and talked them into buying it. Later, when they needed more space, the Bruckners also bought Gurdon Hubbard's The Lilacs next door.

Charlotte Bruckner Sweeney Schmitt related that even before Prohibition, her mother was a teetotaler. Mrs. Bruckner dreaded the idea that people seeing her on the porch of the cottage would think that she was Mrs. Hennessey, the wife of a manufacturer of spirits.

"Mr. Bulkley, a wholesale grocer of Grand Rapids, has bought the Johnson cottage and is occupying it this season. Mr. Bulkley is building a fine barn on the Johnson property purchased by him."

Daily Resorter, August 29, 1885

No other man had a greater influence on the history of both Chicago and Mackinac Island than Gurdon Saltonstall Hubbard. The first meat packer, the first vessel owner, the first lumber dealer, and the first underwriter of Chicago was also the first resort developer of Mackinac Island. Coming west in 1818 when only sixteen years old, he was a founding father of Chicago and the developer of the area of Mackinac Island known as Hubbard's Annex to the National Park. His biography is perhaps the most colorful of anyone associated with Mackinac Island cottages.

Born in 1802 in Vermont, Hubbard left school to contribute to the family finances when he was thirteen. His father Elizur Hubbard, a lawyer, had experienced serious financial setbacks and the loss of his clients. Hoping to start over, the Hubbards moved to Montreal, but Elizur Hubbard found he had to wait out a five-year residency period to practice law there. To supplement the meager income his father was able to earn as a clerk, Hubbard took a job as a clerk in a hardware store. There he met William Matthews, a recruiter and buyer for John Jacob Astor's American Fur Company. Hubbard persuaded Matthews to hire him as a clerk in the Indian country, and he persuaded his parents to let him go on such a dangerous mission. Hubbard agreed to a five-year contract for one hundred and twenty dollars a year.

Leaving Montreal on May 15, 1818, the party of voyagers and clerks reached Mackinac Island on July 4. John Jacob Astor had established Mackinac Island as the headquarters of the American Fur Company. Here in the summers, Astor's traders brought the furs they had

accumulated over the previous winter, collected their pay, re-provisioned, and assembled crews for the next season. Clerks in the warehouses sorted the furs, counted and recorded them, then baled them into ninety-pound blocks for shipping to the East. This was Hubbard's first trip to Mackinac Island, but it created such an impression on him that he returned over and over for business and pleasure.

In September, the Company dispatched Hubbard and a brigade to Illinois where they arrived in Chicago on October 1, 1818. Chicago at that time consisted of Fort Dearborn, the log cabin of John Kinzie, the log storehouse and residence of the American Fur Company's agent John Crafts, and another cabin of Antoine

Gurdon Hubbard at The Lilacs credit Charlotte Ernster collection

Gurdon Hubbard's The Lilacs

porated Chicago in 1835, it designated Gurdon Hubbard as one of the five trustees. Hubbard is even responsible for the physical location of the heart of Chicago remaining near Fort Dearborn at State Street and the Chicago River. When the commission to establish the Illinois and Michigan Canal was considering the northern terminus of the canal, it favored the point where the Calumet River entered Lake Michigan. Hubbard pointed out that since this was within a few hundred yards of the Indiana border, the great city that would grow up at the terminus would be only partly in Illinois. The Illinois-funded commission saw his point and kept the expected city in Illinois.

Hubbard was a director of the State Bank of Illinois, Chicago branch. He was an incorporator of the Chicago Hydraulic Company that built the Lake Street pumping station. In 1836, he wrote the first insurance policy issued in Chicago for the Aetna Insurance Company and carried on an insurance agency until 1868. Hubbard helped organize the Chicago Board of Trade in 1848. He was part owner in two lines of steamers and vessels that plied the Great Lakes. Abraham Lincoln was a personal friend, and Hubbard supported his candidacy for President.

Amidst all this activity, Hubbard married Elinor Berry of Urbana, Ohio in 1831, but sadly she died in 1838. They had one son, Gurdon S. Hubbard, Jr. In 1843, Gurdon, Sr. married Mary Ann Hubbard, his cousin. Gurdon and Mary Ann were

Ouilmette. It is unlikely that Hubbard could foresee the explosion in population of Chicago in such a short period of time ahead, but it is known that he was "spellbound and amazed at the beautiful scene" before him. Nor could Hubbard have predicted the depth of his involvement in Chicago's growth. Indeed, Hubbard's biography is the history of early Chicago.

Hubbard fulfilled his five-year contract with the American Fur Company, then signed on for another two years to command the Illinois brigade at a salary of $1,300 per year. He ultimately purchased the entire interest of the American Fur Company in Illinois. During Hubbard's years as a fur trader, he experienced hardships and adventures with great personal bravery. He once told his nephew that he "did not know the sensation of fear, as he had never experienced it."

He earned the respect of the Indian tribes among whom he traded. He learned their languages and skills. The Indians named him Pa-pa-ma-ta-be, the "Swift Walker," because of his reputation as a rapid traveler on foot. During these years, and even later, this six-foot tall man dressed in a buckskin hunting shirt with a belt, in which he carried a knife, a tomahawk, and a pouch for his flint and steel. He wore moccasins and, sometimes in winter, a red knit cap, although he usually did not cover his long hair. Hubbard remained personal friends with a number of Indians for many years.

As the fur trading waned, Hubbard began trading other commodities. He obtained the contracts to provide beef and pork to the soldiers at Fort Dearborn. The Chicago meatpacking industry began. Gurdon Hubbard was the largest packer in the West for many years.

When the Illinois legislature incor-

devoted to each other. Hubbard affectionately called Mary Ann "Wifey," but she called him "Mr. Hubbard," in the formal manner of many wives of that time. Mary Ann was known as "Aunt Ann" to her nieces and nephews. Gurdon and Mary Ann Hubbard adopted a daughter, Alice.

Throughout these years of success, Hubbard returned to Mackinac Island. In 1855, he bought eighty acres of the Davenport Farm on the southwestern bluff of the Island for $3,000. The amount paid for the land would have been inconsequential to Hubbard at the time.

In 1868, when he was sixty-six years old, Hubbard began to suffer some crippling financial setbacks. In that year, his large meatpacking plant was destroyed by fire. The loss of two of his ships, the *Superior* and the *Lady Elgin*, came as serious financial blows. Perhaps to find some relief from these problems and the summer heat of the city, in 1870 the Hubbards built a small cottage on their land on Mackinac Island. This is the cottage they called The Lilacs. After the great fire of 1871 destroyed Hubbard's China tea-importing enterprise, the Mackinac land and cottage were about all they had left. Hubbard retired from active business, almost.

After the Civil War, people began to flock to healthful resort areas like Mackinac Island. Industrialization made the cities unpleasant in the summer. Those who could afford to escape did so, and that category of people increased in number. By 1875, to protect the Island and to meet the rising demand for recreational areas, Congress created the Mackinac Island National Park. When requests for leases of national park land to build private residences were not acted upon by the government, Gurdon Hubbard, now with failing eyesight but not failing vision, found himself once again in position to profit.

In 1882, Hubbard borrowed money to survey and plat the eighty-acre Davenport Farm to create a resort community. He divided the land into one hundred twenty-nine small lots, named the development Hubbard's Annex to the National Park, and created The Mackinac Island Summer Resort Association. The following year, Hubbard hired experienced and efficient cottage contractor Charles W. Caskey to build the Eating Hall, a community dining room for the Association. The resort community was an instant success. Caskey built nine more cottages in Hubbard's Annex in 1883. The community grew to fifteen cottages surrounding The Lilacs before Gurdon S. Hubbard, fur trader and businessman, died September 14, 1886.

The Lilacs remains a tribute to this incredible man. Since it was originally built in 1870, owners have added a wing to the north and enclosed the south end of the porch. The new north wing has a gabled roof dormer to match the original one on the south. The window in the front gable became a door and the front door became one of three windows. The porch was expanded to accommodate the rearranged entry. The remodeled building followed the Caskey tradition of cottage design, but lacks applied Carpenter Gothic ornamentation.

Mary Ann kept the cottage on Mackinac for many more years, usually renting it out for the season or a part of the season. Her daughter, Alice (Mrs. E. W. Williams), and her granddaughter spent time there, too.

"Mrs. G. S. Hubbard of Chicago is again at 'The Lilacs' after an absence of two years. Her husband, Gurdon S. Hubbard, deceased, was well known among the early residents of the Island. Mr. Hubbard was for many years connected with the American Fur Co. and spent a large part of his life in that work. In 1880 [sic] he purchased the 'Davenport Farm' and laid it out in lots, upon which he built 'The Lilacs.' This was the first cottage on the 'Hubbard annex,' but others were soon to follow among which are those of Michael Cudahy, Dr. L. L. McArthur, William A. Day, Col. Hennessy, Col. Davis, and many others. There are several other very desirable lots to be obtained in this delightful locality."

Daily Resorter, July 23, 1901

The Maples, later known as Star Cottage

McCourtie Cottage
William and Fanny McCourtie — 1883

William H. and Fanny C. McCourtie had Charles W. Caskey build this cross-gabled vernacular cottage for them in 1883. Much of the original Carpenter Gothic ornamentation has been lost. Gone are railings and a bracketed second-story balcony on the east side of the cottage. The bargeboards on the gables remain the same. The porches have been screened.

The McCourtie family was one of five original Annex families from Kalamazoo where McCourtie was a wealthy flourmill owner. In 1867 he was in business with Daniel Merrill. Their business extended beyond just flour milling; they sold village lots and insurance policies, too.

The McCourties did not come to the Island all summer every year. The *Daily Resorter* reported that by 1885, they were renting the cottage to W. Hughart, president of Grand Rapids & Indiana Railroad. Before the 1895 season, the McCourties sold it to George and Susan Miller, also of Kalamazoo. The Millers enjoyed ownership for five years, then James F. and Ellen C. Macauley of Detroit purchased the cottage. While they may have owned the property, the Macauleys rented it extensively.

Among other nationally famous cottagers on Mackinac Island was Supreme Court Justice William R. Day, who rented this cottage from the Macauleys for many years before finally buying it in November 1920. Justice Day had a long history on Mackinac Island, so it not surprising that he brought his family here summer after summer.

William Rufus Day was born in 1849 into a family of judges. His father, Luther T. Day (1813-1885), and his brother Robert H. Day, were both Ohio Supreme Court justices. His great grandfather, Zephaniale Swift, served as a Supreme Court justice in Connecticut. Like his parents, William and his bride, Mary Schaefer, honeymooned on Mackinac Island.

William and Mary brought their four sons to the Island year after year, but they were grown before Justice Day bought a cottage. Oldest son, William L. Day, Jr. became a federal court judge. Luther Day practiced law for fifty-three years in northeastern Ohio as a trial and corporation attor-

credit Clarke Historical Library

ney. According to his February 8, 1965 *Cleveland Press* obituary, "'Lute,' as he was known to his friends, backed up his opinions with logic that rolled forth in oratory that held courtroom attendants spellbound." Rufus and Steven were their other two sons.

Back in Canton, Ohio, their hometown, the Days were neighbors and friends of William McKinley. When McKinley was elected President of the United States, William R. Day served as his Secretary of State. When McKinley was assassinated in 1901, Day was brought in to handle the arrangements. The year that Day was appointed a Supreme Court Justice, 1903, his son Luther married McKinley's niece, Ida McKinley Barber. Luther and Ida Day acquired the Frank Clark cottage across the road after Mr. Clark died in 1919 (see Annex Cottage 5). Justice Day served on the U. S. Supreme Court in Washington for nineteen years, stepping down from the bench the year before he died.

Justice Day died in this cottage on Mackinac Island in 1923.

"Judge William K. [sic] Day, of Canton, Ohio, former secretary of state under the late President McKinley, will occupy the Miller cottage on the Annex again this season. Judge Day is one of the oldest frequenters of the Island; he came here on his wedding journey as did also his father before him. His wonderful record as secretary of state and particularly his work at Paris in completing terms of settlement with Spain entitle him to highest rank as a statesman and a diplomat."

Daily Resorter, July 11, 1902

18 WELLS COTTAGE
HEZEKIAH and ACHSAH WELLS

The Hezekiah and Achsah Wells cottage that William C. Caskey built in 1883 remains one of the best surviving examples of the thousands of summer cottages Caskey built in northern Michigan. It is a symmetrical, cross-gabled vernacular cottage decorated with applied Carpenter Gothic ornamentation, such as scroll sawn railings and a lacy openwork bargeboard. A modern photo of the cottage is not included here. This cottage has changed so little in appearance and the surrounding vegetation has grown so much that the 1883 construction photo remains the best image available. In the early photo, the rear lean-to portion of a typical Caskey cottage can be clearly seen.

The Wells tucked their little cottage between the similar McCourtie cottage and the bluff-side Stockbridge/Cudahy mansion. As the old Davenport farm has re-forested, the cottage has become a very private site with no view of it from any public area.

A view of the cottage may not be available, but the history of it is. Hezekiah G. Wells was born in Steubenville, Ohio in 1812 but moved to the Michigan Territory as a young lawyer in 1833. Wells married Achsah Strong in 1840. They did not have any children of their own, but in their later life, they took great interest in young adult friends. In 1834 Wells was admitted to practice law in Michigan. For the next fifty years, he used his law license mainly in public service, holding public office and serving on various public boards.

Most notable of Wells' public service was his appointment by President Ulysses S. Grant as presiding judge over the "Alabama Claims." During the Civil War, England had permitted the Confederacy to outfit numerous privateers in Britain's ports. These pirate ships had caused damages to the United States. A Geneva conference awarded the U. S. over nine million dollars. Wells served as judge in Washington, D. C., hearing over 2,068 of the damage cases and ordering payment on the claims. In 1856 Abraham Lincoln was a little known politician from Illinois. Wells invited Lincoln to visit Kalamazoo on behalf of the Republican candidate for president, John C. Fremont. Lincoln came and made his only Michigan speech.

In 1883 Hezekiah and Achsah Wells joined four other prominent families from Kalamazoo who built cottages in Hubbard's Annex on Mackinac Island. Judge Wells was only alive to enjoy two seasons at this cottage. In about 1903 Hugh and Fannie Patrick bought the Wells cottage. Patrick was a Chicago physician, a specialist in mental and nervous diseases. They had two children who came to the Island with them, Talbot and Catherine. Mrs. Patrick's father was Judge Joseph E. Gary, a Chicago superior court judge for forty-three years. Judge Gary sat on the bench longer than any other jurist in Cook County. In many elections, both political parties nominated him.

Francis Stockbridge already owned the site for a grand hotel he envisioned on Mackinac Island when he and Betsey built this magnificent cottage. At their home in Kalamazoo, they entertained lavishly, and this cottage was built for lavish entertaining as well. Stockbridge was one of the successful lumber barons of the era. He was open-hearted, whole-souled, generous, majestic and courtly. But he was also approachable; popular with everyone, especially his own employees; pleasant; congenial; of gentle humor; and level-headed.

Francis Brown Stockbridge was born in 1826 in Bath, Maine. He entered the business world at sixteen, leaving home to clerk in a dry goods store in Boston. He soon moved to the exciting frontier town of Chicago where he opened a lumberyard and began amassing a fortune in this business. These were the years of the "big cut." Virgin timber covered the land and would be cleared for farms. Stockbridge made a wise move to Saugatuck, Michigan, Allegan County, closer to the trees, after making valuable business contacts during his years in Chicago.

In Saugatuck, Stockbridge built a number of saw mills at the mouth of the Kalamazoo River with partner Otis R. Johnson (see Annex Cottage 14). The mills turned out millions of board feet of lumber. He met and married a local girl, Elizabeth Foster Arnold, better known as Betsey. They had one child, a son Joseph, who died in infancy while they lived in Saugatuck. Betsey was somewhat eccentric, dignified, and austere, but she was loved by all who knew her.

Stockbridge also began his politi-

FRANCIS and ELIZABETH STOCKBRIDGE
LAKE CLIFF
1884

cal career during these years, serving in the Michigan legislature from 1869 until 1873. He was distinguished not only as a keen businessman, but also as a skilled organizer, and as a calm, insightful, and prudent manager. By the 1870s, lumbering operations were moving north. Stockbridge and Johnson relocated their lumbering op-

"Col. Stockbridge's elaborate cottage built on a knoll on the edge of the bluff and his billiard hall clinging to the side of the precipice, affords a view almost unequalled in the north... and no trouble or expense has been spared to add to the attractiveness and comfort of the place."

Daily Resorter, August 16, 1887

erations to St. Ignace on the Upper Peninsula of Michigan, closer to the trees. They formed the Mackinac Lumber Company and the Black River Lumber Company, both of which Stockbridge served as president. At the same time the lumbering operations left Saugatuck, the Stockbridges relocated their residence to Kalamazoo. The Stockbridges' home, large and stately, served as a center of Kalamazoo's social and political activity.

Stockbridge and his brother-in-law, George T. Arnold from Allegan County, both became involved with Mackinac Island. George began the Arnold Line ferry company (see Lakeshore Cot-

tage 8). Stockbridge bought land on the southwest side of the Island with a commanding view of the Straits of Mackinac. He envisioned the grandest hotel in the world built on that site.

In the meantime, Francis and Betsey joined four other elite families from Kalamazoo and partner Otis R. Johnson from Racine, Wisconsin, in Gurdon Hubbard's Annex to the National Park. Stockbridge surely knew Hubbard from as far back as his days in Chicago in the late 1840s. Here was a choice site on private land to build a cottage, while the National Park lagged behind in issuing leases for building sites. Just west of the hotel site, this lot had nearly the same commanding view of the straits. A more elaborate structure, the Stockbridge cottage was not completed until the following year, 1884.

Stockbridge wanted the hotel built, and he was a keen businessman, keen enough to know that he was a lumberman with no expertise in the hospitality business. So while Stockbridge was the moving spirit behind the Grand Hotel, he arranged to have no financial interest or risk in it. Stockbridge persuaded the transportation lines that terminated at Mackinaw City to create this destination for passengers. The Michigan Central Railroad,

Grand Rapids & Indiana Railroad, and the Detroit & Cleveland Navigation Company steamship line formed the Mackinac Hotel Company, a stock corporation, to build the hotel on the site Stockbridge sold them. The corporation hired a hotel management company to operate it.

Stockbridge's sale of land was contingent upon the hotel suiting him. He rejected deals because the plans for the hotel were not elaborate enough. Finally they all accepted the design of George Mason of Detroit. The company hired Charles W. Caskey to execute the plans. Caskey was the logical choice as the builder of the Grand Hotel. The thirty-seven-year-old contractor had the crews, the equipment, the materials, the skills, and the reputation to build a one thousand-guest hotel with a six-hundred-foot long front porch in time for the 1887 summer season. Caskey was also from Allegan County, Michigan, the same as Stockbridge's wife, brother-in-law, and Stockbridge's early lumber empire.

Caskey and three hundred workers built the Grand in less than four months using 1.5 million board feet of lumber and hauling supplies from the mainland across the ice late in the winter. The Hotel opened on schedule on July 10, 1887.

While the Grand Hotel may be the best-known monument to Stockbridge, institutions throughout the Great Lakes states may also serve as such. The Stockbridges gave enormous amounts of money to charities: Kalamazoo Children's Home, the YMCA, Academy of Music, a Chicago hospital, Kalamazoo College, and the Kalamazoo Opera House, among others.

The year 1887 was a busy year for Stockbridge. He bought and re-organized a spring works as Kalamazoo Spring and Axle Company, of which he was president. He became involved with west coast lumber interests through a son of Otis R. Johnson, Charles Russell Johnson, in the Ft. Bragg Lumber Company. Stockbridge diversified into iron mines in Menominee. While he was in Menominee, he formed the Menominee River Lumber Company as well. A lover of fine horses, Stockbridge had an interest in race horses at S. A. Brown & Company, a stock breeding farm in Kalamazoo. As if this were not enough, Stockbridge returned to politics and was elected U. S. Senator. He had little time to relax on the porch of the cottage overlooking the Straits of Mackinac.

Just as they had been the center of society in Kalamazoo, the Stockbridges held a prominent social position in Washington, D.C. They moved in the most select circles and were noted for their entertaining and receptions. Betsey was known for her elegant wardrobe and jewelry in Washington. She particularly favored heavy white satin and had many gowns she never wore as she preferred her older ones.

Realizing that they had so little time to spend on Mackinac, the Stockbridges sold this cottage in late 1889 to another larger-than-life, successful businessman, Michael Cudahy. Betsey's brother George and his family were full time residents, and nephew George Stockbridge had a West Bluff cottage. Either of them could provide the Stockbridges with ample accommodations when they could find the time to be on the Island.

Francis Stockbridge was elected to another term in the Senate in 1893. That July he visited Mackinac for what was probably the last time. In April 1894, he died in Chicago on his way to a California vacation with Betsey. After his death, Betsey traveled and spent several winters at their home in Washington, visited her home in Kalamazoo in the summer, and visited her brother on the Island. She moved to the Island with her brother permanently in 1904 and spent the last seven years of her life there under his care. She died on Mackinac at George Arnold's house in August 1911.

Cudahy extensively remodeled the original Stockbridge cottage into a Queen Anne. Which owner built the four-story round tower with the conical roof remains a mystery. The tower's open-air fourth floor looks out over the Straits of Mackinac.

This cottage is the first of two owned by Michael and Catherine Cudahy on Mackinac Island. The sale included the original furnishings, and for the $7,000 purchase price, Stockbridge also agreed to build a dock and a footpath down the bluff to it. The Cudahys traveled by boat from their dock to Mass at St. Anne's Catholic Church on Sundays while they summered here. Michael Cudahy sold this cottage to his brother Edward in 1897, developed land in California for several years, and then after returning from this business venture, built the palatial Tudor Revival residence, Stonecliffe (see Lakeshore Cottage 20).

WEISS COTTAGE

1905 JOHN AND MARGARITE WEISS

John Weiss was the successful president of the Gottfried Brewery in Chicago when he had local contractor Patrick Doud build this Colonial Revival cottage in 1905. Weiss immigrated to Chicago from Germany in the 1880s and quickly advanced in the Gottfried Brewery. Through mergers, Gottfried became one of the largest breweries in the State of Illinois. Owner Matheus Gottfried and his daughter Margarite were impressed with Weiss. In 1884, Weiss and Margarite Gottfried married. When Matheus Gottfried retired in 1892, he designated son-in-law Weiss as president of the brewery while his own son, Karl, served as secretary.

The Weisses had two teenage sons, Norman and John Herbert, when they moved into their cottage. They may have also brought with them from Chicago some of their servants who included Louisa and Annie, from Germany; Marie, from Canada; Edith, a Belgium tutor; and Andrew, the German coachman, with his wife Lena and their children, Edith, Clara, and Andrew. The cottage is certainly large enough to accommodate them all!

The Weisses sold the cottage in 1916 after enjoying it for twelve years. John Weiss died three years later. Mrs. Weiss and their two sons moved to Arizona.

Hubert Burnham, his wife Vivian, and their daughters, Cheryl and Mardi, of Chicago became the next owners of the cottage. Hubert Burnham worked in the architectural firm of his father, Daniel Burnham, a renowned architect responsible for much of today's Chicago skyline and waterfront park design. Daniel Burnham also oversaw the architectural aspects of the Columbian Exposition in Chicago in 1893. This connection may account for the unsubstantiated report that the cottage was originally built as an exhibit for the Columbian Exposition, dismantled, and shipped to Mackinac, where it was said to have been reconstructed by Doud. The eleven-year gap between the Exposition and the construction of the cottage also makes this story unlikely.

Neighbor Dr. Lewis Linn McArthur, prominent Chicago surgeon and quite possibly Mrs. Burnhams's regular physician, performed an emergency appendectomy on Mrs. Burnham. This emergency surgery occurred before there was an Island medical facility and pointed to the need for one.

The main part of the cottage is a symmetrical three-story structure. An Ionic portico prominently fronts the north façade. Gabled dormers project from atop the gambrel roof. A Palladian or fanlight transom surmounts the front side-lighted double doors. A Palladian window on the third floor highlights each end of the structure. The south façade has another Doric portico and is intersected by a one-story columned veranda that surrounds the cottage on three sides.

Colonial Revival followed the Victorian styles and emerged in the 1880s. The style borrowed heavily from early American architecture. It reflected a new pride in America's past and a growing interest in historic preservation. The design incorporated characteristics of Colonial buildings such as Palladian windows, gambrel roofs, pedimented porticos, columns, and classical detailing. Colonial Revival structures are much larger than their historic counterparts. Spacious rooms with large windows allow a cheery brightness in the rooms not found in the smaller, darker rooms of the Victorian period.

The kitchen wing appears to have been added on to the cottage at

a later time; however, an inspection of the structure reveals a simultaneous construction. The cottage would certainly have been built with a kitchen as the Annex Eating House had already ceased operation before this cottage was built. The kitchen may have been in the separate wing to minimize fire danger and to keep the house cooler.

An early exterior photo of the house shows small trees screening the kitchen wing, so that only the main house is visible from the road. Those trees have grown and tower over the roofline; their trunks do not hide the kitchen wing like the greenery once did.

credit Sharon Hahn collection

Mackinac Island

Lake Shore and More Cottages

N

The Cottages

1. Governor's Residence
2. Corner Cottage
3. Lakewood Cottage
4. Werner Tea Room
5. Villa Du Lac
6. Windermere
7. Anne Cottage
8. Brigadoon
9. Yacht Club
10. Bonnie Doon
11. Small Point
12. St. Croix
13. Silver Birches Lodge
14. Silver birches Cottage
15. Point aux Pins
16. Early Cabin
17. McNeill Cottage
18. Hanna Cottage
19. Packard Cottage
20. Stone Cliff

Lake Huron

Point Aux Pins

British Landing

Lake Shore Road

British Landing Road

Crooked Tree Road

Leslie Avenue

Sugar Loaf

Sugar Loaf Road

Stonecliffe Shore Road

Stonecliffe Road

Garrison Road

Annex Road

Hoban Road

Custer Road

Arch Rock Road

Lake Shore Road

Park

Grand Ave.

Annex Road

Pontiac Trail

West Bluff Road

Grand Hotel

Grand Avenue

Huron Road

Fort Street

Fort Mackinac

Huron Road

Huron Street

Mahoney

Market Street

Lake Shore and More

Beauteous isle, I sing of thee,
*   Mackinac, my Mackinac;*
Thy lake-bound shores I love to see,
*   Mackinac, my Mackinac!*

From Arch Rock's heights and Shelving Steep
*   To Western cliffs and Lovers' Leap,*
Where memories of the lost one sleep,
*   Mackinac, my Mackinac!*

Attributed to Robert Clark, 1892

This chapter presents eighteen cottages that fringe Mackinac Island's eight-mile shoreline, beginning and ending at two additional inland mansions, both designed by architect Frederick Perkins. Starting at the prominent and stately Michigan Governor's Summer Residence near the Fort, circle the Island counter-clockwise, past Colonial Revival mansions, Queen Anne confections, rustic log cabins and lodges, to the palatial Tudor Revival estate known as Stonecliffe. Some of the cottages are on private land; others are on leased state park land with only the structures owned by private individuals. Windermere, Small Point, and Stonecliffe are open to the public for overnight accommodations. One cottage serves as the Mackinac Island Yacht Club.

1 GOVERNOR'S RESIDENCE
LAWRENCE and MABEL YOUNG 1902

Lawrence and Mabel Young had been married for eight years when they moved into their new Mackinac Island cottage with their children: Henry, Alice, and Robinson. Early in their marriage, the Youngs had relocated from Lawrence's hometown, Louisville, Kenturcky, to Chicago, Mabel's hometown. Chicago contributed significantly to the prosperity that enabled them to build this elegant summer cottage.

Young was born in Louisville where his father, Colonel Bennett H. Young, was a distinguished Confederate officer and a noted lawyer. While at Princeton University, Lawrence Young pitched on the baseball team for four years and captained the team his senior year. He graduated in 1892 and enrolled in law school at the University of Louisville, conveniently close to his father's law practice, which he joined upon graduation in 1893.

Louisville, Kentucky is well known for its horses and its horse races. Perhaps through their mutual interest in horses, Young met and married Mabel Wheeler in 1894. Her father, George Henry Wheeler, was president of the Washington Park Club, the best known race track in America. Young later served multiple terms as president, and also chaired the Western Jockey Club for five years. The latter organization controlled all racing in the West and South, setting racing dates and disciplining all jockeys and horse owners.

Wheeler was president of the Chicago City Railway Company. Young joined his father-in-law in the company, serving as vice president, then as director upon Wheeler's death. Young continued to practice law and was appointed assistant corporation counsel for the City of Chicago for a term.

Young hired a fellow member of the Washington Park Club and the Saddle and Cycle Club, architect Frederick W. Perkins, to design a residence for the beautiful west fort lot that he and Mabel had leased from the Mackinac Island State Park Commission. Perkins had attended Massachusetts Institute of Technology, then furthered his studies in architecture at L'Ecole des Beaux Arts in Paris. He began his own architectural firm in Chicago in 1888. By 1901, he was well qualified for Young's assignment. Perkins later designed Stonecliffe for Michael Cudahy (see Lakeshore Cottage 20).

The cottage Perkins designed is reminiscent of the transitional Shingle Style, fading by 1901, but hints of the

"Mr. and Mrs. Lawrence A. Young, of Chicago, are now located in their cottage, having arrived last Tuesday. Since last summer, Mr. Young has had an elegant new cottage built, just west of the Fort, at the top of the bluff, overlooking the village and harbor. It is an ideal spot, giving a beautiful view of the water for many miles around, as well as of the town. The cottage itself is one of the most beautiful ones on the Island, with an immense veranda extending across the front of it and running back some distance on each side. Within, it is very elegantly and tastefully furnished, and when fully completed, as it will be in a few days, will make an exceedingly beautiful and elegant summer home. Mr. and Mrs. Young expect to entertain this week, Mr. Robert Wheeler, of Chicago, Mrs. Elizabeth Young, of Louisville, and Mrs. W. W. Goodrich, of Harbor Springs, all of whom will arrive Wednesday on the Manitou."

Daily Resorter, July 1, 1902

evolving Arts and Crafts style. This is evident in the large hipped roof with dramatic flaring eaves. Gabled dormers with similar flaring eaves project from the roofline. The walls and roof are finished with wood shingles, once painted a dark color to blend with nature. The foundation walls and chimneys are native limestone. Situated alone on a projecting knob of the bluffs, immediately west of Fort Mackinac and 125 feet above Lake Huron, the dormer windows and wide verandas provide a sweeping view of the Straits of Mackinac.

Local Mackinac contractor Patrick Doud supervised a large crew of seventy-five craftsmen to execute Perkins' design over the winter of 1901-1902. Doud contracted to complete the project for $15,000; however, Mable paid Doud a bonus of $500 to express her delight with her new summer residence.

Mabel died in her early forties on July 15, 1915, at the cottage that so delighted her. Fellow Mackinac cottagers Dr. Lewis Linn McArthur, from Chicago and Hubbard's Annex, and Milton Tootle, Jr., from St. Joseph, Missouri and the East Bluff, mourned her passing, honoring her as pall bearers at her funeral in Chicago.

Eight years later, Lawrence Young married Mrs. Sarah Caldwell Smith. One year later, at age fifty-four, he died. Clara and Hugo Scherer of Detroit bought the cottage in 1926. They sold it in 1945 to the Mackinac Island State Park Commission for use as the Michigan Governor's Summer Residence. The Park paid the Scherer family $15,000, the same price the Youngs paid to build it.

Lawrence and Mabel Young with children credit Mackinac State Historic Parks, Michigan

Charles and Hattie (Kimble) Anthony built this spacious cottage in about 1899, but they had been regular cottagers on Mackinac Island since before 1887. They owned a double cottage, with Charles' younger brother, Clifford M. Anthony, called Windermere (see Lakeshore Cottage 6) on Biddle Point, a short distance to the east from this location. After more than ten years sharing a cottage, it was time to build their own due to two significant events in the Anthony families—Charles' retirement and the birth of a child to Clifford and Flora, his wife of three years. Each brother built a new cottage (see Lakeshore Cottage 3) and sold their double cottage that in a few short years would become the now-famous Windermere Hotel.

The Anthony brothers were investment bankers from Peoria, Illinois. Of the Anthony Loan and Trust Company, Charles was president and Clifford was vice president. They specialized in bonds and first mortgage loans for farmland in the Corn Belt of Illinois, Iowa, Nebraska, and Missouri. By 1893 the volume of their business was greater than that of any other investment bankers in the West. Despite thirty-eight years and a high volume of business, never did one of their clients foreclose nor one of their investors lose a penny. In addition to the bank, the brothers owned the Peoria Safe Deposit Company, a companion business. Charles and Hattie Anthony's only child, Earl C.

CORNER COTTAGE

CHARLES AND HATTIE K. ANTHONY 1899

Anthony, left the Island a legacy of even greater historical significance than this lovely cottage. They likely indulged this child with their wealth because two older sons died before Earl's birth. In 1900, after his parents moved into their new cottage, nineteen-year-old Earl brought his locomobile to the Island. Autos had been banned on village streets since 1898, but not in the Park. One summer day while driving in the Park, Earl's locomobile frightened several horses, causing injury to them and wrecking a number of carriages. The accident caused such an uproar that the Mackinac Island State Park Commission followed the village's example and banned automobiles from the Park as well. Mackinac Island remains one of the only places in the United States free of motor vehicles.

This two-story structure is built in the Colonial Revival style of architecture that enjoyed a brief period of popularity from 1890 to 1910. A prominent characteristic of this style is a hipped roof, here accentuated by a central gable with a Palladian window. Smaller twin gables are paired with the main gable. A central bay window below the main gable maintains the symmetry of the cottage. Such balance is a relief from the extreme asymmetry of the earlier Victorian styles.

A front porch supported by six columns extends along the entire front of the cottage. Many similar porches on Mackinac were enclosed for additional multi-season living space. But for the delicate Chippendale-inspired railing, this one remains wide open to the sweeping view of the straits and the boardwalk.

About 1914, while the Anthonys lived in Los Angeles, near Earl and his wife Irene (Kelly) Anthony, Charles died. In 1918, Hattie sold the cottage to J. A. and Esther Beck of Jefferson County, Iowa.

3 CLIFFORD AND FLORA ANTHONY 1899 LAKEWOOD COTTAGE

Clifford and Flora (Thomas) Anthony built this spacious cottage in about 1899, following the July 9, 1898 birth of their only child, Emerson Thomas, on Mackinac Island. Clifford had been a regular cottager on Mackinac Island since before 1887. He owned the double cottage called Windermere with his brother Charles. Clifford and Charles shared the cottage for more than ten years. However, after Charles retired and Clifford and Flora were married and had Emerson, the brothers decided to build separate cottages.

Clifford and Charles Anthony already jointly owned a number of lakeside lots. This land transferred to Clifford in late 1898 and the Corner Cottage lot (see Lakeshore Cottage 2) was transferred individually to Charles.

This two-and-a-half story symmetrical cottage features a veranda that runs the full width of the structure. Together with the ample windows grouped in threes and projecting from gabled dormers, it affords the occupants access to fresh breezes and pleasant views.

The Anthony brothers were investment bankers from Peoria, Illinois. Of the Anthony Loan and Trust Company, Charles was president and Clifford was vice president. They specialized in bonds and first mortgage loans for farmland in the Corn Belt of Illinois, Iowa, Nebraska, and Missouri. By 1893 the volume of their business was greater than that of any other investment banker's in the West. In their thirty-eight years of operating a high-volume business, never did one of their clients foreclose nor one of their investors lose a penny. Clifford remained president of the company after Charles' retirement in 1898. Just before Clifford retired in 1905, the company consolidated with Dime Savings of Peoria. In addition to the bank, the brothers owned the Peoria Safe Deposit Company, a companion business.

Shortly after Clifford Anthony retired, he and Flora sold this cottage to Martin and Agnes Shaughnessy of St. Louis on August 29, 1906.

Ransom W. and Libbie (Viger) Hawley of Detroit built this cottage along the Lake Huron shore in about 1891 and enjoyed it until 1919. In 1916, Ransom W. Hawley retired as a partner in the firm of Thorpe, Hawley & Company, a candy distribution company in Detroit. Libbie Hawley was the daughter of Captain Edwin R. Viger, one of the founders of the Detroit & Cleveland Navigation Company, a partner in the Grand Hotel. Their family home was on Farmer Street, the site later occupied by the J. L. Hudson department store in Detroit. No children survived Ransom's death at age seventy-three in 1922 or Libbie's death at age seventy-five in 1929.

Herman B. and Coral E. Werner operated the Werner Tea Room from 1926 to 1950 serving dinners to tourists and cottagers during the summer season.

The ornate six-sided tower with oval windows quickly draws the viewer's attention to a simple intersecting-gabled Carpenter Gothic cottage. The tower was originally shorter, but raised during a cottage expansion project. Above the main first-story porch, the front gable shelters a porch on the second floor.

WERNER TEA ROOM

1891   RANSOM AND LIBBIE HAWLEY

JOHN AND KATE SAMUEL VILLA DU LAC

"C.M. Richards, cashier of the First National Bank of Urbana, Ohio, is passing a couple of weeks with his mother, Mrs. Amelia I. Richards, at 'Villa Du Lac Cottage' on the Lake Shore Drive."

Daily Resorter, July 28, 1894

John B. and Kate M. Samuel, of Peoria, Illinois, owned this lot from 1889 to 1900, the years when construction of this cottage was most likely. The Mackinac Island Historical Register records them as the builders. John Samuel was the secretary and manager of Title Guaranty, Abstract & Trust Company of Peoria, Illinois and most certainly a business associate of cottage neighbors, Charles E. and Clifford M. Anthony, also bankers from Peoria. The construction date of 1891 is assumed correct since the cottage to the west, known as the Werner Tea Room (see Lakeshore Cottage 4) also claims that date of construction, although 1900 is another possible construction date.

The property clearly transferred to Amelia I. Richards in 1900, a widow who retained the property in her name until 1922. It is possible that she had the cottage built although Charles and Hattie Anthony signed a warranty deed to Amelia I. Richards on August 15, 1900. Mrs. Richards was to have possession of the property on November 1, 1900. Three weeks later after the August transfer, John and Kate Samuel of Los Angeles signed a quit claim deed for the same property to Charles E. Anthony to clear the questionable transfer.

Support for the theory that Charles Anthony built the cottage is that on the backs of two large Victorian beds and dressers on the second floor of the cottage are tags with the name "Anthony" written on them. The furniture could not have come up the stairway and into the bedrooms after the cottage was completed. They could have been raised into the rooms through the front double windows before the windows were set.

Architectural details of

Victorian era styles have been added to a simple Carpenter Gothic cottage. As part of a major remodeling project in the mid-1980s, eight feet were added to the west side of the cottage along with the ornate tower, a third floor dormer, and bay win-

dows. A two-sided oriel window replaced the small square casement at the front peak. Another one enhances the addition's peak on the rear side. The original porch was also enlarged. These changes further confuse determining the date of construction by visual inspection as these enhanced features make it appear older than it may be.

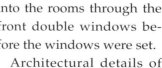

above left: Villa du Lac before the 1980s remodeling
above right: Villa du Lac after the 1980s remodeling
credit Clayton and Anna Timmons collection

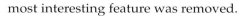

THE ANTHONY BROTHERS

WINDERMERE

1887

Charles E. and Hattie (Kimble) Anthony, with his younger brother Clifford M. Anthony, built this double cottage called Windermere on Biddle Point in 1887. Richard Rickman, from the Anthonys' hometown, Peoria, Illinois, designed and built the cottage. It has grown in every direction, including up, since its construction as the first Queen Anne cottage on the Island. The contrasting paint colors on lacy openwork trims, rails, and spandrels are gone. Solid and dignified columns have replaced the delicate and ornate porch posts. From the third level of a lighthouse-style tower, atop of which flew the flag, cottagers could watch the arrivals and departures of boats in Mackinac Island's harbor; however, this most interesting feature was removed.

The Anthony brothers were investment bankers. Two years prior to building the cottage, they sold their interests in the Washington, Illinois firm of Anthony & Denhart and their interests in the Illinois Bank of Chatworth in order to move the farm loan operations to Peoria, Illinois. They formed the company C. E. & C. M. Anthony, Investment Bankers and the Peoria Safe Deposit Company. When they incorporated in 1891, the bank became the Anthony Loan and Trust Company with Charles as president and Clifford as vice president. The bank specialized in bonds and first mortgage loans for farmland in the Corn Belt of Illinois, Iowa, Nebraska, and Missouri. By 1893 the volume of their business was greater than that of any other investment bankers in the West. In their thirty-eight years of operation in a high-volume business, never did one of their clients foreclose nor did one of their investors lose a penny. Clifford became president of the company after Charles' retirement in 1898 and remained president until he retired in 1905 when the company was consolidated with Dime Savings of Peoria.

For a few years, the two Anthony families came to the Island with their horses early in the summer season and stayed late into the fall. Then, other destinations called them in the summers, too. In 1893, Clifford Anthony, still a single man, came to the Island in late July after "an extensive European tour" and stayed at the Grand Hotel. The following season, newspaper accounts indicate the Anthonys rented Windermere to two other families.

Clifford Anthony and Flora Thomas, half his age, wed in November

1895 and may have spent the summer at Windermere as newlyweds in 1896. They certainly spent the next summer there as their only child, Emerson Thomas, was born on Mackinac Island on July 9, 1898. The same year, Charles Anthony retired from active participation in the business.

In about 1899, the two brothers built single-family dwellings on lakeshore land they owned just west of Windermere (see Lakeshore Cottages 2 and 3). According to newspaper accounts, they sold Windermere to the Westhimer family. In 1904, Islander Patrick Doud bought the cottage.

Patrick Doud was a cooper, making barrels during the Island's fishing era when fish and everything else was packed in barrels instead of cardboard cartons for shipping. The fishing industry and barrel making gradually faded as the Island's tourism and building industry grew, along with the Island building trades. Doud turned his skill with wood into building cot-

"Messrs. Charles and Clifford Anthony of Peoria, Ill., who own and occupy the handsome double cottage 'Windermere,' on the Point, will remain on the Island until about October 1st. They come early, bring their horses, and by staying late getting the benefit of the most enjoyable month in the season."

Daily Resorter, August 30, 1887

"Ferdinand Westhimer and family of St. Joseph, Mo., and Morris F. Westhimer, of Cincinnati, are at their cottage 'Windermere' for the season. The Messrs. Westhimer are the distillers of the famous 'Red Top' and 'Boston League' brands of wet goods".

Daily Resorter, July 3, 1901

tages, homes, and businesses on the Island. He built the Young cottage, now the Governor's Summer Residence (see Lakeshore Cottage 1), Stonecliffe for Michael Cudahy (see Lakeshore Cottage 20), the Tootle cottage (see East Bluff Cot-

tage 10), and the Weiss cottage (see Annex Cottage 20). He also entered the hotel business by converting the Anthony's double cottage into the Windermere Hotel that continued to be operated by his descendants for over a century.

credit Mackinac State Historic Parks, Michigan

7 1899 ALVIN AND SALLIE HERT ANNE COTTAGE

Anne Cottage is one of three cottages in a row along the waterfront below Fort Mackinac that the Park began to develop in 1897. This prime location between the old Indian Dormitory used for the Island schoolhouse and the Island House Hotel, was the site of the old Indian Agency House that burned in 1870. In 1895, the State of Michigan took over the National Park operations, and its budget needed a boost. Leasing more land, as on the East and West Bluffs, could provide more revenue.

The Mackinac Island State Park Commission platted and leased the three additional lots for at least $100 per year. It required that cottage construction begin within one year of signing the lease and that the cottages be worth more than $3,000. In May 1899, Alvin T. and Sallie A. Hert signed the lease for this lot.

Alvin Tobias Hert, known as "Tobe," grew up along the Ohio River in Owensburg, Indiana. He was the son of a general store owner. Sallie was from nearby Bedford. Tobe worked as a traveling salesman for a shoe manufacturer until he settled down in Brazil, Indiana. There he established his own general store and became involved in politics. The citizens elected him mayor of Brazil in 1895, when

Anne Cottage as originally built in 1899 credit Mackinac State Historic Parks,

he was thirty years old. That same year, the State appointed him superintendent of the Indiana Reformatory at Jeffersonville. Four years later, the Herts were following their dream of a summer cottage on Mackinac Island, building Anne Cottage.

The name Anne Cottage comes from the Constance Fenimore Woolson novel *Anne,* set on Mackinac Island and involving the old Indian Agency House, once on this site. The popular author was the great-niece of author James Fenimore Cooper, who wrote the classic *Last of the Mohicans.* In 1916, Samuel Mather and his sister placed a tablet in memory of Constance Fenimore Woolson, just east of Fort Mackinac and near V. W. Mather's East Bluff cottage, Crow's Nest (see East Bluff Cottage 1).

In 1904, Tobe organized the American Creosoting Company in Shirley, Indiana. The railroad companies that creosoted railroad ties to preserve them were his major customers. Hert's company grew to fifteen plants and subsidiaries.

The hip-roofed Colonial Revival cottage with broad overhangs grew in floor space as the Herts became more affluent. A major expansion of the cottage occurred in the early 1900s. Its new horizontal emphasis gave it a Prairie style appearance. The cottage features a broad ample front porch. Two stories rise over a native stone foundation.

Perhaps the Herts grew weary of the high traffic location of Anne Cottage. In 1915, they bought the country estate Stonecliffe (see Lakeshore Cottage 20) from the Cudahy heirs. Michael Cudahy had owned a magnificent Annex cottage overlooking the Straits of Mackinac (see Annex Cottage 19). He moved to California to develop real estate, and then he returned to the Island, building Stonecliffe in 1904. The Herts socialized with the Cudahys on the Island, but Michael Cudahy died in 1910. The neighbor next door to Anne Cottage, Susan B. Arnold, took the lease on Anne Cottage.

On June 7, 1921, Tobe was "smitten by apoplexy" and died while attending a meeting of the Republican National Committee, being held in his hotel room in Washington, D.C. Sallie took up the reins, serving as chairman of American Creosoting and vice chairman of the Republican National Committee from 1924 to 1935. President Herbert Hoover strongly considered Sallie for the cabinet post of Secretary of the Interior.

"A. T. Hert of Jeffersonville, Ind., arrived on the island yesterday and is busy getting his beautiful cottage Anne in readiness for immediate occupancy. Mrs. Hert is expected to arrive today."

Daily Resorter, July 19, 1902

Anne Cottage in the early 1900s credit Mackinac State Historic Parks, Michigan

8 1899 GEORGE and SUSAN ARNOLD
BRIGADOON

The name Arnold is well known on Mackinac Island. The Arnold Transit Company is the oldest shipping company on the Great Lakes, transporting passengers to Mackinac Island on the Arnold Line ferry for over a century. This is the home of its founder, George T. Arnold. In about 1899, George and Susan Arnold built this home. It is the only residence on leased park land built as a year-round residence, not as a summer cottage, although later owners have used it exclusively in summers.

George T. Arnold was born in Allegan County, Michigan, the younger brother of Elizabeth Foster Arnold who would become Betsey Stockbridge, the wealthy socialite of Kalamazoo, Mackinac Island, and Washington, D.C. George and Betsey's father, Dan Arnold, was one of the earliest settlers in Allegan County. George Arnold started out as a fisherman. In 1876, he won appointments as Saugatuck Postmaster and as Deputy Collector of Customs. His association with sister Betsey's husband, Francis Stockbridge, took him to Mackinac Island. Francis Stockbridge operated lucrative sawmills at Saugatuck, but when logging was exhausted there, he relocated to St. Ignace as the Mackinac Lumber Company. This venture got Arnold to the Straits area where, with L. B. Coates, also of Saugatuck, they began a shipping business in 1878, with an order of ten barrels of fish. Arnold and Coates used other steamers at first, then purchased their first boat in 1883. That same year, the Stockbridges built an Island cottage in Hubbard's Annex near the land Stockbridge purchased as the site of the Grand Hotel (see Annex Cottage 19). First servicing the lumber and fishing industries, Arnold's business turned more to transporting tourists and supplies for them.

Arnold soon bought out his partner and painted Arnold Line Steamers on the bows of his fleet. He incorporated the Arnold Transit Company, Inc. in 1900, about the time he moved into this cottage.

In 1895, just after the death of his brother-in-law, who was to begin a second term as U. S. Senator, Arnold was appointed one of five commissioners to the new Mackinac Island State Park Commission. He held the position until 1903, serving twice as acting park superintendent when the commission had no funds to hire anyone else to do the job. Serving as acting park superintendent had other advantages than salary. Arnold was on the committee that platted these three lots for lease, and he applied for one of them himself in 1899.

The Arnolds built this large fashionable Queen Anne summer house on their lot close to the docks from which they could oversee operations. The house possesses all the ingredients of a fine summer retreat—asymmetry, tower, wrap around porch, bays, dormers, and native materials. The unmistakable three-story round tower with a bell roof greets arrivals in the harbor as it has for over a century. Stone pillars rise from the ground to support delicate columns that in turn support the wide curving veranda.

From this house, Arnold enlarged the company, merged Arnold Line Steamers with Arnold Transit, and gave passengers another reason to ride his ferry by partnering in the Chippewa Hotel in 1902. The widow Betsey came to live with the Arnolds here in 1904, dying in this home seven years later. On September 16, 1921 at age seventy-five, George T. Arnold died of a massive stroke. Susan Arnold took over the leadership of this well known Island institution, Arnold Transit.

"Fourteen years ago Geo. T. Arnold and L. B. Coats came here with a fishing tug and a ton of hustle apiece. They rented a little shed... and went in for blood. First thing people knew, they had a dock and it wasn't many years before they had another one. Then Arnold got ambitious and bought out Coats."

Daily Resorter, August 25, 1893

above: The logo of Arnold Transit company credit Arnold Transit Company

9 WILLIAM & ESTELLE HITCHCOCK YACHT CLUB
1901

While it has been known as the Mackinac Island Yacht Club since 1937, this cottage was originally the summer residence of William E. and Estelle Hitchcock. By 1901 when the Hitchcocks signed their lease for this park lot, Mr. Hitchcock was in the forefront of business activities in their hometown, Muncie, Indiana. His Muncie Skewer Company manufactured butchers' skewers at a daily capacity of over one million. Perhaps this venture brought Hitchcock into contact with the Chicago meat packers on the Island.

He served on the board of directors of various banks, a newspaper publishing company, the country club, the electric company, the interurban railway, and the police commission. In 1901, he was elected vice president of the National Manufacturers Association of Indiana and appointed a member of the governor's staff.

Estelle, known as "Minnie," and William had three sons; however, only William E. Hitchcock, Jr. survived childhood to spend his adolescent summers on Mackinac Island. In 1907, the Hitchcocks moved from this cottage to the East Bluff (see East Bluff Cottage 6), away from the busy main street of the town and near the cottages of other Hoosiers.

BONNIE DOON
1886
TRUMAN & EMMA JEAN BROPHY

The Grand Hotel was still only a plan when Truman W. and Emma Jean (Mason) Brophy of Chicago started building their cottage, Bonnie Doon, in 1885. A few other families had already built summer cottages in Hubbard's Annex and East Bluff, but the Brophys chose this lot in the village. The small but fanciful pitched roof porch has been replaced by a more practical shed roof entry; however little else has changed on the front façade of Bonnie Doon from the time that the four Brophy children, Truman, Jr.; Jean; Florence; and Alberta ran in and out of this door. Over one hundred years later, the two-story tower continues to hug the corner of the intersecting gable cottage.

Truman W. Brophy, medical doctor and dentist, born April 12, 1848, was a pioneer in oral surgery. A visit from an itinerant dentist to the family farm when Truman was twelve years old provided his earliest inspiration to become a dentist. The itinerant dentist's work fascinated him. Dr. Brophy would later say that his first work as a dental assistant was to hold this man's horse.

Of even greater inspiration to Dr. Brophy were the thousands of children born with cleft lip and cleft palate for whom the leading orthopedic surgeons of the day said correction of the condition was impossible. Dr. Brophy became obsessed with a desire to devise a procedure to correct this most conspicuous deformity. Already a successful dentist, he decided that medical school was necessary to achieve this goal.

Dr. Brophy's plans were delayed, however, when Emma Jean Mason came to his attention. While walking along Monroe Street in Chicago one day in 1872, he noticed a lovely dark-eyed girl in a black velvet gown seated in a Victoria drawn by a splendid matched pair of black horses. Instead of attending Rush Medical College that winter, the twenty-four-year-old spent

"Dr. T. W. Brophy, of Chicago, has bought the lot opposite Mrs. Todd's, and will erect a fine double cottage this fall."

Daily Resorter, August 29, 1885

Dr. Truman Brophy and one of his favorite teams, credit: Truman W. Brophy Memoirs

the term at Martine's Dancing Academy with Miss Mason. They were married the following spring. Dr. Brophy graduated from Rush in 1880 as president of the class. He performed his first cleft palate surgery, with great success, in 1886, the year after they built their Mackinac cottage.

Truman Brophy organized the Chicago College of Dental Surgery, and he served that institution as professor of oral surgery and as dean for about forty years. In 1923, it became the Loyola University Dental School.

Brophy was also one of the first to notice the connection between mouth cancer and tobacco. In a 1915 study of men afflicted with that mouth disease, he reported that all of them were smokers.

On August 8, 1921, Dr. Brophy and Frederick B. Moorehead, also of Chicago, met with Dr. Henry Sage Dunning, of New York at the Chicago Athletic Club to organize the first association in North America of specialists in what would come to be called plastic surgery.

"Scottish names seem to be favorite and no wonder for their rugged syllables enclose a wealth of tender sentiment. Besides 'Cairngorm' [on West Bluff] there is 'Craigmawr,' which means 'high bluff,' owned by Mrs. James Walsh of Chicago and 'Bonnie Doon' occupied this season by Mr. and Mrs. A Weiter of Indianapolis, Indiana, first built by Dr. T. W. Brophy of Chicago and named in honor of her parents who lived upon the veritable 'banks and braes of Boonie Doon.'"

Daily Resorter, July 28, 1894

Instead of coming to Mackinac Island, the Brophys more often went to their summer home in Lake County, Illinois where Truman maintained a stable of trotting horses in which he took great pride. Emma Jean died in 1898, and Truman sold Bonnie Doon.

Dr. Brophy married Esther Strawbridge of Philadelphia in 1908. They traveled extensively to medical and dental conferences around the world and had a second home in California. Dr. Brophy continued his life's work for another twenty years, writing a book on oral surgery, then another on clefts of the lip and palate while performing a greater number of surgeries than each year before. He was seventy-nine when he died on February 4, 1928 in Los Angeles.

ALANSON & ANN SHELEY
SMALL POINT
1882

Alanson and Ann Sheley's cottage originally sat up on the bluff to the southwest from its present location on Lake Shore Road. It was moved in the 1950s when Moral Re-Armament (MRA), an international organization led by Frank Buchman and dedicated to a program of "moral and spiritual rearmament," developed a conference facility at Mission Point.

The Sheley cottage demonstrates many elements of Gothic Revival, a style that was popular elsewhere earlier than the construction date. Gothic Revival was one of the first Victorian building styles to become popular; however, no buildings on Mackinac Island survive from this period and style. The absence of Gothic Revival structures here may be the result of the economic depression experienced on the Island while the style was most popular in Michigan. That period coincided with the demise of fur trading and commercial fishing, but came before the tourist era returned prosperity to the Island.

This style is characterized by vertical or perpendicular accents. Steep roofs, tall and pointed windows, and rich embellishment with carved wood to simulate the stone tracery characteristics of Gothic churches are typical of buildings from this period.

Alanson Sheley was born in 1809 in Albany, New York and grew up on his grandfather's farm. When he was still a boy, he took a raft of timber down the St. Lawrence River, shooting the rapids, and sold it for a good price when he safely reached Quebec. At sixteen, Sheley began an apprenticeship as a stonemason and builder, soon becoming a skilled craftsman. He was employed as a foreman in the construction of the Rideau Canal in Canada. Moving to Detroit in 1831, before Michigan was a state, his first building contract in Michigan was for the erection of a lighthouse at Thunder Bay on Lake Hu-

"Allanson Sheely [sic], of Detroit, celebrated his 78th birthday at his cottage at Mackinac last night. The grounds were illuminated with Chinese lanterns, there being 78 upon the house, and a grand display of fireworks was given from Robinson's Folly and 100 guests received elegant refreshments served on the veranda."

Daily Resorter, August 16, 1887

120

ron. In 1835, he married Ann Elizabeth Drury, and he became the general manager of the Black River Steam Mill & Lumber Company. He remained in that position for twenty years. Sheley then became a member of the wholesale drug firm, Jacob S. Farrand & Company.

Sheley served Detroit and Michigan in various official capacities, including two terms in the state senate. He owned substantial holdings of real estate in Detroit and Port Huron, as well as an interest in the Detroit & Cleveland Steam Navigation Company, a partner in the Grand Hotel. The Sheleys summered in this cottage for five years before the hotel was built in 1887.

The Sheleys were early members of the First Presbyterian Church of Detroit, serving in positions of church leadership for many years. Perhaps through this connection, they purchased land at Mission Point from the Presbyterian missionary organization that operated the Mission House in the 1820s.

Alanson Sheley's seventy-eighth birthday party was typical of the elaborate celebrations held on the Island, with fireworks and exotic Chinese lanterns. It is unlikely that the elegant refreshments served to the one hundred guests included any intoxicating beverages; Sheley was a "brave defender of the cause of temperance" and refrained from drinking alcohol or using tobacco throughout his life. At seventy-eight, he was still going strong, six feet tall and two hundred and seventy-five pounds. Sheley was known for his physical strength. He died five years later, preceding Ann in death by just a year.

credit Mackinac State Historic Parks, Michigan

12 1904 ROLAND HUGHES
ST. CROIX

Roland and Lena Hughes bought this land on St. Clair Point from John Early, an Island farmer. They bought it to build St. Croix Cottage, their Island retreat. They built the barn first, in 1904, giving the horses the better accommodations for the first three years. The Hughes followed the common practice of staying in tents until they could develop their cottage. The simple American foursquare cottage, built in 1907, was in great contrast to their magnificent home in Cygnet, Ohio and to the grand summer houses found elsewhere on the Island.

The cottage has changed little over the years as the Hughes, and later their niece Alice wanted to keep it always the same. The ample porch, so necessary to resort living, originally extended the full length of the front and side of the house, partly enclosed by glass. The corner was later enclosed to expand the interior living space. A windmill to pump water from Lake Huron has been removed from the yard.

Roland Hughes and Helena L. Martin were both born in Maine. Hughes' father was a farmer, but he had died when Hughes was sixteen. Hughes and Martin married young, then set out together to seek their fortunes in the west. Starting as a day laborer in the Pennsylvania oil fields, Hughes saved enough to start a general store with a small stock of merchandise. By 1890, the Hughes' successful involvement in oil production took them to Cygnet. They opened another general store, produced oil extensively in Ohio and Kentucky, started a coal business largely operated by Lena Hughes, and then established an electric power plant. They owned extensive real estate.

By 1899, with oil operations extended to Illinois, Oklahoma, and Kansas, Roland and Lena Hughes organized the Cygnet Savings Bank. Roland Hughes served as president until he died in 1925. Lena Hughes was deeply involved in the bank, regularly influencing its policies.

While successful in business, the Hughes had no children. When she was quite young, Lena Hughes' niece Alice (Mrs. Carl Schwyn) began to live with them. Alice was eight when the barn on Mackinac Island was built, and the family camped on the property. The cottage remained hers until her death in 1973. Subsequent owners renamed the cottage Easterly. Visitors should respect private property and not enter the gate.

credit Candace and Brian Dunnigan

SILVER BIRCHES LODGE
1907–1912
13

Mrs. Edna W. Troop bought this parcel from Island farmer John Early and his wife Kate, in late September 1906. Early had inherited half of the 636-acre farm that included this land from his father, Michael Early, in 1895. Doing business as the Langham Hotel Company, Mrs. Troop soon erected this two-and-a-half-story Adirondack lodge. It is a rustic log structure with a gabled roof and five gabled dormers across the front. Eight log posts in front and four more on each end support a two-story veranda. Shingles clad the upper portion of the lodge.

Troop took a mortgage, possibly to finance the construction of three satellite cottages in 1912, but failed to pay. Troop's hotel dreams ended. In 1914, the Lincoln National Life Insurance Company of Ft. Wayne, Indiana foreclosed and got a court order to sell the lodge at an auction.

Finding a buyer took six years. It was the end of 1920 when J. A. and Esther Beck bought Silver Birch Lodge. The Becks were from Jefferson City, Iowa and previously owned Corner Cottage on Lakeshore Drive (see Lakeshore Cottage 2) for two summers. They sold Corner Cottage in the fall of 1919 at a quick $5,000 profit. The property records do not indicate what they paid Lincoln for Silver Birches.

E. M. Tellefson, who operated a radio and telegraph station for the Great Lakes shipping industry at Fort Holmes, located high on the Island, bought the property from the Becks in the fall of 1930 at the beginning of the Great Depression.

Tellefson rolled one of the three satellite cottages over the ice to leased land in the Park (see Lakeshore Cottage 14). He is notorious in Island history for having a car that he boldly drove from this remote location to the radio station in the early 1930s, years after automobile were banned from operating on the Island. He finally complied with a court order to stop driving the car, and he stored it on the Island for forty years.

It has been said that Fred Hasselbun, for the Sullivan Steamship Line, built the log lodge in 1905, however, this is not verified by the public record of land transfers.

right: Silver Birches Lodge and Guests
credit Mackinac State Historic Parks, Michigan

14 1912 SILVER BIRCHES Cottage

E. M. Tellefson, who operated a radio and telegraph station for the Great Lakes shipping industry at Fort Holmes, located high on the Island, bought Silver Birch Lodge in the fall of 1930 (see Lakeshore Cottage 13). In about 1932, Tellefson rolled one of the three little Silver Birch satellite cottages over the ice on logs to this leased land in the Park.

Mrs. Edna W. Troop and her Langham Hotel Company built the cottage on the original location in about 1912, but the venture was not a success. The Lodge and the cottages sat in foreclosure for six years.

Visitors should respect the privacy of the cottage occupants and not climb the stairs to the cottage.

top: E.M. Tellefson's Silver Birches Cottage
bottom: Two of the Silver Birches Cottages remaining on site with the lodge.

15 POINT AUX PINS

EDWARD AND STEPHANIE GOTT

The cedars of Point aux Pins danced to the music of Franz Schubert for the many years the illustrious musician's great niece summered here. Stephanie K. Ortman Gott was born in about 1864 at Gmunden, the Austrian summer resort village in which Schubert spent much of his life. Her grandmother was Schubert's sister. Mrs. Gott was devoted to the music and memory of Schubert, collecting portraits and memorabilia of the famous composer until she had the largest collection of its kind in the world. Some of it she kept at her home in Detroit, but part was here, where she was hostess to various musicians and students.

An even greater tribute to Schubert was Gott's devotion to his music. An accomplished musician, Gott played Schubert's compositions at many recitals and taught them to hundreds of her students at the East Side Settlement House in Detroit, to which she was also devoted. After the 1904 suicide of her attorney husband, Edward A. Gott, Mrs. Gott began to volunteer at the community center. There she established the Sophie Wright Day Nursery, named after a New Orleans social worker, and served as president of the organization. In 1913, she established the Franz Schubert Music Settlement, a program at the settlement house to teach music lessons to hundreds of children for a small fee. Gott also directed the settlement string orchestra.

Mrs. Gott came with her family to Saginaw, Michigan when she was four years old. Her father, Edgar Ortman, was involved in the lumber industry and served as mayor of Saginaw. She married Edward Gott in 1886. They had one son, Edgar N. Gott. Edgar was just five when the family began to summer on Mackinac Island, a tradition that Gott would keep for forty years. She died at this cottage from a stroke in 1933. Mrs. Gott is buried on the Island.

Two rustic cottages of unpeeled cedar logs with massive stone fireplaces hide behind the over grown cedars and a rustic fence. Major J. Hudson Poole of Detroit once owned the other rustic cottage. It has not been occupied since 1935. Poole was no relation to Samuel B. Poole, the Mackinac Island State Park Superintendent from 1898 to 1903 and owner of the Iroquois Hotel. The two cottages remain virtually unchanged since they were constructed earlier than 1919. The land is leased from the state park, and its records do not indicate a more precise construction date.

E. M. Tellefson (See Lakeshore Cottages 13 and 14) bought these cottages in the early 1940s. The family occupied only the Gott cottage but Tellefson bought them both because they are so close together and he did not want neighbors.

16 MICHAEL EARLY 1910 EARLY CABIN

Michael Early was a farmer on the Island. In 1860, he and his wife Mary bought a 636-acre farm, roughly the north east quarter of Mackinac Island. They paid $5,000 to an heir of Michael Dousman, who had carved the farm out of the forest fifty years earlier. The Early family grew hay and vegetables on the farm.

By 1870, the Earlys built an Italianate house on the 1814 Battleground near the center of the Island to replace the Dousman house. The Park tore down the Early's Italianate house in the 1950s.

After Michael Early's death, the property was passed down to Michael and Mary's sons, Peter and John. The sons continued to farm, but also sold some of the desirable lakeshore property to summer cottagers. The Earlys also built a lakeshore cottage of their own, The Bungalow, where it was cooler for the summers.

Peter Early leased the central part of the farm to a group of cottagers for a golf course. Golfers at the Wawashkamo Club on British Landing Road now play through Early's fields.

The simple two-story cabin of large saddle notched logs rises to a gabled roof. A porch extends the full breadth of the house.

17 McNeill Cottage

Henry and Fannie McNeill   1912

Fannie (Rison) McNeill's mother, Julia Cherry Rison, had recently died in January 1911 when thirty-seven-year-old Fannie bought this property for a cottage from farmer John Early late in the summer. Perhaps the funds were her inheritance from her mother, but Fannie probably took five years to pay John Early as the deed was not recorded until 1916.

Fannie was from Paris, Tennessee where her husband Henry C. McNeill owned McNeill Brothers Grocery with Frank McNeill and was also a partner in Paris Tile Flooring and Roofing with a group of prominent Henry County, Tennessee citizens. Henry and Frank McNeill were both members of the "Porter Guards," a contingent of honor guards under Tennessee Governor James D. Porter. Fannie's father, Joseph Rison, was a hotelkeeper, just off the court square in Paris.

It is likely that Fannie hired Island contractor Patrick Doud to build this simple cedar log and cedar shingle one-and-a-half story cabin with a stone fireplace. On a board of a built-in seat in the cottage is written "Patrick Doud."

In 1952, seven years after Henry died and when Fannie was seventy-eight, she transferred the cottage to her niece, Frances Walker Rison Lagerquist. The transfer may have been premature as Fannie lived to be ninety-four. Only three people owned the cottage in ninety years, the third reclaiming it from the cedar forest that had begun to grow through cracks in the floor *inside* the cottage after Frances stopped maintaining it.

18 ALEXANDER & ELIZABETH HANNAH
HANNAH COTTAGE
1905

Alexander W. Hannah spent many summers on Mackinac Island before building this cottage in 1906, but in quite a different setting. His parents, Alexander D. and Catherine Hannah built the cottage Cairngorm on the West Bluff in 1887 (see West Bluff Cottage 6), then remodeled it into one of the finest Queen Anne summer houses on the Island in 1892. This remote, rustic cottage at British Landing was built in sharp contrast to his parents' showplace.

Elizabeth Hannah studied the metaphysical teachings of the Rosicrucian Order and wrote the book *Dawn of a New Day* during the years at this cottage. The Rosicrucian Order provides a systematic approach to the study of higher wisdom that empowers one to find the answers to questions about the workings of the universe, the interconnectedness of all life, one's higher purpose, and how it all fits together. She left the copper plates for the book in the cottage when they sold it in 1909 to Elisha and Mary A. Morgan of Lake County, Illinois.

The first level of the cottage is cedar log. Three sets of multi-paned double-hung windows stretch across the cedar-shingled walls of the second floor above a central entry. A stone chimney and a paper birch split log stairwell complete the rustic style of the cottage. A devastating tornado in 1994 dropped trees on all sides of the cottage but left the main structure untouched while the carriage house with a 1905 carriage inside it was demolished. The clapboard and shingled beach house also survived the tornado.

right: The beach house to Hannah Cottage

GEORGE & CAROLINE PACKARD 1902
19 PACKARD COTTAGE

Caroline's mother, Frannie Jane Howe, talked George and Caroline Packard, of Chicago, into buying this piece of land from Island farmer Peter Early in November 1901. Frannie Howe first vacationed on Mackinac when the Civil War ended. The "Fairy Isle" enchanted her.

An architect friend, Henry Barker, from George Packard's eastern hometown designed the cottage. The Packards hired Island contractor G. W. Dewey and his son to build it. They had the lumber floated across Lake Huron from St. Ignace. That may have been one of the last deliveries of lumber to the Island made in that manner.

The wide central front stairway beckons visitors to sit on the porch that stretches across the entire front side. The solid board porch railing matches the lower level siding of the cottage for a unified appearance. Three cedar-shingled dormers each feature double windows.

George and Caroline Packard's older daughter Polly was born the same year the cottage was built. From here the Packards watched the sunsets over St. Ignace and hiked the mile and a half to Point Aux Pins for a view of the northern waters.

Caroline was a Chicago native. Her parents Francis and Frannie Howe moved there from New England for Francis to work with his uncle, Gurdon Hubbard, pioneer of Chicago and developer of Hubbard's Annex on Mackinac Island. George was a New Englander, too, born in Providence, Rhode Island and educated at Brown University. He came to Chicago to attend Northwestern University Law School. Instead of returning east after his graduation in 1891, he stayed in Chicago to marry Caroline in 1893 and live in the same house together for over fifty-seven years.

George Packard, a prominent Chicago attorney, spent his legal career with the firm Peckard, Brown & Packard, serving as assistant attorney for the World's Columbian Exposition in 1892-1893. George died in 1949, passing the Mackinac cottage on to future generations of Packards.

Stonecliffe estate reigns as the largest of the historic summer cottages on Mackinac Island. Built by Michael and Catherine Cudahy in 1904 on 150 acres, Stonecliffe is situated toward the interior of the Island rather than by the water's edge. Michael Cudahy, one of five brothers, sold his sizeable Queen Anne cottage in Hubbard's Annex (see Annex Cottage 19) to his brother Edward in 1897 and headed for California to develop a tract of land. Returning from this business venture, he hired Chicago architect Frederick Perkins to build the palatial Tudor Revival residence. Perkins demonstrated his ability two years prior by designing the Lawrence Young cottage (see Lakeshore Cottage 1) near Fort Mackinac, now the Michigan Governor's Summer Residence.

Michael, as well as his brothers, Patrick, Edward, John, and William (although William died at an early age) were self-made men, finding prosperity in Chicago's meatpacking industry. Michael was a partner with Philip Danforth Armour, then the leader in the competitive meat packing industry. By 1892, Michael and Edward established Cudahy Packing Company with main offices in Omaha, Nebraska. Michael Cudahy established the practice of moving meat on refrigerated wagons, a novel idea that transformed the business from seasonal to year-round. He was regarded as a pioneer in business with a reserved, studious, and quiet, yet social, disposition. He took great inter-

1904
STONECLIFFE
MICHAEL AND CATHERINE CUDAHY

est in sports and was a lover of fine arts, especially music.

Michael Cudahy was born in Callan County, Kilkenny, Ireland in 1841 to Patrick and Elizabeth (Shaw) Cudahy. Suffering the pangs of hunger during Ireland's potato famine, the family boarded the ship *Goodwind* and headed for America. Michael was eight years old on that journey. His brother John was six, sister Catherine was three, baby Patrick was not yet one, and infant Anna died on the

passage. Michael's brothers, William and Edward, were born in Milwaukee in 1853 and 1860, respectively. Michael began working at a neighbor's slaughterhouse at age fourteen and learned the bloody side of the business. From there he never faltered in his ambition or imagination.

Michael Cudahy and Catherine Sullivan married in 1866 and had seven children, four boys and three girls. Michael's health began to fail in 1910, and he died at his Chicago home in Novem-

credit Mackinac State Historic Parks, Michigan

133

ber. He ended his days as a multi-millionaire with a stately home in Chicago and a mansion on Mackinac Island, the epitome of the American rags to riches story. His legacy is well known in Cudahy, Wisconsin and Cudahy, California, towns he and his brothers help establish. One of the recipients of his many charitable donations was Loyola University in Chicago where $130,000 funded the Michael Cudahy Science Hall. Loyola University was also the recipient of Edward Cudahy's endowment for a library in memory of his wife, Elizabeth.

In 1915, Alvin Tobias and Sallie Aley Hert bought Stonecliffe from the Cudahy heirs. That same year they erected another smaller version of the Tutor Revival on the property for entertaining their guests. The guesthouse contains its own bowling alley. Since 1899, the Herts had owned Anne Cottage below the Fort (see Lakeshore Cottage 7). Perhaps the Herts grew weary of the high traffic location of Anne Cottage.

Alvin Tobias Hert, known as "Tobe," grew up along the Ohio River in Owensburg, Indiana, the son of a general store owner. Sallie was from nearby Bedford. Tobe worked as a traveling salesman for a shoe manufacturer until he settled in Brazil, Indiana. There he established his own general store and became involved in politics. The citizens elected him mayor of Brazil in 1895, when he was thirty years old. That same year, the State appointed him superintendent of the Indiana Reformatory at Jeffersonville. In 1904, Tobe organized the American Creosoting Company in Shirley, Indiana. The railroad companies that creosoted railroad ties to preserve them were his major customers. Hert's company grew to fifteen plants and subsidiaries.

On June 7, 1921, after owning Stonecliffe for only six years, Tobe was "smitten by apoplexy" and died while attending a meeting of the Republican National Committee being held in his hotel room in Washington, D.C. Sallie took up the reins, keeping Stonecliffe another twenty-six years and serving as chairman of American Creosoting and vice chairman of the Republican National Committee from 1924 to 1935. President Herbert Hoover strongly considered Sallie for the cabinet post of Secretary of the Interior. Shortly before her death in 1948, Sallie Aley Hert deeded the Stonecliffe estate to the Episcopal Cathedral Foundation of Washington, D. C.

The Tudor Revival style of Stonecliffe was derived from English Renaissance half-timbered buildings of the sixteenth century. They are typically asymmetrically massed with steeply pitched roofs and one or more intersecting gables, as evidenced in Stonecliffe. The cottage also features gabled roof dormers, decorative half-timbering, decorative quatrefoils, a recessed main entry way, and a round tower. Islander Patrick Doud was likely the general contractor.

The Cudahy family in front of Stoneciff during construction credit: Michael and Jane Bacon collection

EPILOGUE

The seventy-three "imposing domiciles" called "cottages" that top the bluffs, circle a quiet neighborhood park, and ring the shoreline of Mackinac Island were built board by board over 100 years ago. Their devoted custodians have celebrated the cottages' one-hundredth birthdays, often with elaborate parties. Part of the daily life of the 500 Island residents, the cottages also greet one million visitors each year. The residents and visitors remember the Fort, The Grand Hotel, fudge, horses, scenic beauty, fresh air, and always, the historic cottages. We hope that this pictorial guidebook has answered the curious questions of resident and visitor alike, "Who built that cottage?"

Why are these cottages such an integral part of the Mackinac Island experience? Why are their owners so devoted to them? Why should anyone care about their history—or their future? We have learned that the cottages are more than old buildings.

We have used the seasonal homes to teach you some Mackinac Island history. The cottages represent the cultural history of an entire era of Island life. Historic buildings help us understand our past, which helps us understand our present and future. The cottages also connect us, over time and with each other. Furthermore, unlike the soul-less sprawl at the edges of cities, the historic cottages of Mackinac Island contribute to the natural beauty of the land. They possess an intrinsic beauty all their own.

A goal of this book is the preservation of the historic buildings of Mackinac Island. We strongly feel that you will be more likely to protect and care about their survival if you know more about them. We hope that you will want to contribute your time and money to their preservation.

The Pompa Fund for Preservation of Historic Strucures is an endowed fund of the Mackinac Island Community Foundation. The Foundation is a non-profit, community corporation that manages a collection of endowed funds, makes grants from these funds for projects that enhance Mackinac Island, and is worthy of your donation. The Foundation also manages the Wilfred Puttkammer Mackinac Island Conservation Fund. Reach the

West Bluff including a view of The Grand Hotel credit Clarke Historical Library

Foundation at P. O. Box 1933, Mackinac Island, Michigan 49757. The authors will donate a portion of the profits from the sale of this book to the Pompa Fund.

Another way to contribute to historic preservation on Mackinac Island is to volunteer time and donate to the Mackinac State Historic Parks. The Park owns and protects, for the public, the land on which West Bluff, East Bluff, Fort Garden, and Point aux Pins cottages are built. The Park leases the land to cottage owners with restrictions to maintain the cottages. Modifications to the cottages must comply with U. S. Department of Interior architectural standards. One way to become involved with the Park is to join Mackinac Associates, a non-profit "friends of the park" organization at P. O. Box 1800, Mackinac Island, Michigan 49757.

The real heroes of cottage preservation are their private owners. Each of the cottages is privately owned and maintained through owner dedication, money, and sheer willpower. The Island's isolation makes even ordinary repairs tremendous obstacles. We applaud the owners and thank them for helping us make this book become a reality. At the very least, do nothing to make their job of cottage maintenance any harder than it is.

The information we have included in *Historic Cottages of Mackinac Island* is only as accurate as we know it to be. Local histories published in the late 1800s and early 1900s, city directories, and census records were major sources of our information. They contained their share of er-

rors and exaggeration, and some of the stories are anecdotal. If we have repeated any of their errors, we apologize, but we feel confident that we have sought in our research the most reliable information available.

One of our greatest fears is that important information may have been

omitted or may be incorrect. Please bring this to our attention. Send corrections and additions for future editions with your name, address, telephone number, and e-mail address to us at Arbutus Press, P. O. Box 234, Mayfield, Michigan 49666, or arbutuspress@traverse.com.

Send us information about other historic buildings on Mackinac Island, too. The summer cottages included here are

not nearly a comprehensive inventory of all the historic residences on the Island. Many of the year-round homes are even older than the summer cottages. Each one would have a story to tell in a companion pictorial guidebook to the historic *homes* of Mackinac Island.

May this book have helped you

enjoy the rich beauty and cultural history of Mackinac Island and inspired you to protect its future.

SELECTED BIBLIOGRAPHY

Alter, Judy. *Stewart Edward White*. Western Writers Series, 1975.

American Biographical History of Eminent and Self-Made Men. Cincinnati: Western Biographical Publishing Co., 1878.

Andreas, A. T. *History of Chicago*. Salem, MA: Higginson Book Co.,1884.

Anthony, Charles Lawton. *Genealogy of the Anthony Family from 1495- 1904*.

Armour, David A. *One Hundred Years at Mackinac*. Mackinac Island: Mackinac State Historic Parks, 1995.

Armstrong, Joe. "The Grand Tale of Francis B. Stockbridge." *Kalamazoo Gazette*, Sept. 30, 1979.

Arnold Transit Company. "Mackinac and the Local Ferryboats." Ms.

Bateman, Newton. *Historical Encyclopedia Of Illinois and History of Peoria County, vol. 2*. Peoria: Munsell Publishing Co., 1902.

Beatty, John D. *Beyond These Stones-A History of Trinity Episcopal Church*. Ft. Wayne, Ind.: Trinity Episcopal church, 1994.

Before the Bridge: History of St. Ignace. St. Ignace, MI: Kiwanis Club, 1957.

Benjamin, Robert. E-mail to author. Dec. 10, 2000; Jan. 11, 2001.

Benser, Robert. Telephone interview. Dec. 27, 2000.

Biographical and Historical Memoirs of Muskingum County, Ohio. Goodspeed Publishing,1892.

Bogan, Jackie. Telephone interview. Aug. 16, 2000.

Bogan, James. E-mail to author. Jan. 16, 2001.

—. Telephone interview. Sept. 6, 2000, Dec. 17, 2000, Jan. 16, 2001.

Bolotin, Norman and Christine Laing. *The World's Columbian Exposition, The Chicago World's Fair of 1893*. Preservation Press.

Bours, Allen L. *Proceedings at the Laying of the Corner Stone of the New Capitol of Michigan*. Lansing: W. S. George & Co., 1873.

The Brewing and Malting Industry of Chicago. Chicago: Reed & Co.

Bronfman, Ann. Telephone interview. Dec. 9, 2000.

"Burial Thursday for Mrs. Hawley." *Detroit News*, Mar. 27, 1929.

Burton, Clarence and Agnes M. Burton, eds. *History of Wayne County and the City of Detroit, Michigan*. Chicago, Detroit: The S. J. Clarke Publishing Co.,1930.

Busch, Jane C., *Mackinac Island National Historic Landmark* Survey, 1999.

Carley, Rachel. *The Visual Dictionary of American Domestic Architecture*. New York: Henry Holt and Company, 1994.

Chicago und Sein Deutschthum. Cleveland, OH: German-American Biographical Pub. Co., 1901. Trans. by Peggy Tuck Sinko.

"Close of a Busy Life, Gurdon S. Hubbard Passes Away." Clipping file. Chicago Historical Society. Sept. 14, 1886.

Collections of the Minnesota Historical Society, vol. III. St Paul, MN: The Minnesota Historical Society, 1898.

Commemorative Historical and Biographical Record of Wood County, Ohio. Chicago: J. H. Beers & Co., 1897.

Compendium of History and Biography of The City of Detroit and Wayne County, Michigan. Henry Taylor & Co., 1909.

Conrad, Howard L. *Encyclopedia of the History of Missouri, vol. 4*. New York: Southern History Company, 1901.

"Cook County, Illinois Census." 1880, 1900, 1910.

Cook, Frederick Francis. *Bygone Days in Chicago*. Chicago: A. C. McClurg & Co., 1910.

Cunningham, Joseph O., ed. *Encyclopedia of Illinois*. Chicago: Munsell Publishing Co., 1905.

Cushman, George F. "The Late Rev. Samuel Smith Harris, D.D., LL.D., *The Churchman*. Sept. 1, 1888.

Daily Resorter [Petosky, Michigan], 1883-1902.

Dau's Detroit Blue Book and Ladies' Address Book. Detroit: Dau Publishing Co., 1901 ed.

Davenport Democrat and Leader, December 15, 1915.

Day, William R. Letter to J. F. Macauley. June 15 1902. Roush collection of cottage memorabilia, Mackinac Island.

"Death Claims Betsey Foster Stockbridge." *Kalamazoo Gazette*, Aug. 29, 1911.

"Death of Mr. Frank M. Clark." *Kalamazoo Gazette*. May 10, 1919.

"Death Takes Mrs. Helena L. Hughes, Cygnet Pioneer." *Daily Sentinel Tribune* [Bowling Green, Ohio], Jan. 25, 1940.

Deed Records. Registrar of Deeds, Mackinac County Courthouse, St. Ignace.

"Delaware, County, Ohio Census." 1880.

Denham, Laura. E-mail to author. Jan. 16, 17, and 23, 2001.

Detroit City Directory. 1919, 1921-22, 1922-23, 1925-26, 1926-27.

Detroit Death Index.

Detroit Free Press, July 14, 1912.

Doolen, Carl. Telephone interview. Dec. 17 and 21, 2000.

Doud, Jeannette. Telephone interview. Feb. 17, 2000; Jan. 4, 2001.

"Dr. Longyear Dies Suddenly." *Detroit Free Press*. June 3, 1921.

"Dr. McArthur, Noted Chicago Surgeon, Dead." Clipping file. Chicago Historical Society. Nov. 6, 1934.

Dunbar, Willis F. *Kalamazoo and How It Grew*. Kalamazoo: Western Michigan University,1959.

Dunnigan, Brian. Telephone interview. Apr. 9, 2000.

Dunnigan, Brian and Candace Dunnigan. Personal interview. Aug. 5, 2000.

Dunnigan, James P. *Around My World in 80 Years*. Privately printed. Dec. 1990.

Durant, Samuel W. *History of Kalamazoo County, Michigan*. Philadelphia: Everts & Abbott, 1880.

Dziabis, Marvin D. Personal interview. June 16, 2000.

Early, William. Telephone interview. Sept. 7, 2000; Jan. 4, 2001.

Eckert, Kathryn Bishop. *Buildings of Michigan*. New York: Oxford University Press, 1993.

Edmonds Tribune-Review [Washington]. Mar. 31, 1933.

Edwards, Richard. *Industries of Michigan, City of Detroit*. New York: Historical Publishing Co., 1880.

Encyclopedia of Michigan. New York, Detroit: Western Publishing and Engraving Co., 1890.

"Ended Life with a Bullet." *Detroit Free Press*, May 10, 1904.

Eraser, Alexander. *A History of Ontario: Resources and Development*. Toronto: Canada History Company, 1907.

Ernster, Charlotte. Personal interview. June 10, 2000.

Erwin, Helen B. Letter to Mrs. F. G. Hammitt. June 18, 1965. Bentley Historical Lib., Ann Arbor.

Faubion, Hazel A. *Tales of Old "St. Joe" and the Frontier Days*. 1977.

Findley, Lois. Telephone interview. Sept. 7, 2000.

Fisher, David and Frank Little, eds. *Compendium of History and Biography of Kalamazoo County, Mich*. Chicago: A. W. Bowen and Co., 1906.

French, Charles, ed. *Biographical History of the American Irish in Chicago*. Chicago: American Biographical Publishing Co., 1897.

"Funeral Services Held for Mrs. Stephanie Gott." *Detroit Free Press*, July 10, 1933.

Gallery, Audrey. Telephone interview. Sept. 13, 2000.

Gilbert, Paul T., Charles L. Bryson, Wallace Rice, and Caroline McIlvaine. *Chicago and Its Makers*. Chicago: F. Mendelsohn, 1929.

Gilpin, John. Telephone interview. Nov. 1, 2000

"The Governor's Summer Residence." Mackinac Island State Park Commission, 1977.

Gram, Nancy Williams. Personal interview. June 10, 2000.

Griswold, Joseph Bert. *The Pictorial History of Fort Wayne, Indiana*. Chicago: Robert O. Law Co., 1917.

Hahn, Sharon K. Letter to the author. Mar. 27, 2000.

Haiken, Elizabeth. *Venus Envy: a History of Cosmetic Surgery*. John Hopkins University Press, 1997.

Haimbaugh, Frank D., ed. *History of Delaware County*. Indianapolis: Historical Publishing Company, 1924.

Hamilton, Alice. *Exploring the Dangerous Trades*. Boston: Little, Brown and Co., 1943.

Hamilton Evening Times [Ontario] , June 30, 1905.

Hamilton, H. R. *Footprints*. Chicago: The Lakeside Press, 1927.

Hannabass, Kitty. Interview by Carl Nold. 1998.

Hirsch, Edwin. *Frank Billings: The Architect of Medical Education, Apostle of Excellence in Clinical Practice, a Leader in Chicago Medicine*. Chicago: The Author, 1966.

History of Buchanan County, 1881. Reprint. Cassville, MO: Seward W. Lilly, 1973.

History of Buchanan County and St. Joseph, Mo. St. Joseph, MO: St. Joseph Publishing Co., 1898.

History of Kent County, Michigan. Chicago: C. C. Chapman & Co., 1881.

Hogg, Victor. *A Survey of the Buildings of Mackinac Island.* Mackinac Island State Park Commission. 1971.

Holt, Fred. Telephone interview. Aug. 15, 2000.

In Memoriam: Founders and Makers of Michigan. Detroit: S.J. Clarke Co., 193-?

Javis, Nancy H., ed. *Historical Glimpses-Petoskey.* Petoskey, Michigan: Little Traverse Historical Society, 1986.

Journal of Commerce. St. Joseph, MO, July 1900.

"Judge Gary Dies 'In the Harness.'" *Chicago Tribune,* Nov. 1, 1906.

"Kalamazoo Man Presiding Judge of Grant's Court of Alabama Claims."*Kalamazoo Gazette*, Jan. 19, 1930.

Kelton, Dwight H. *Annals of Fort Mackinac.* Detroit: Detroit Free Press, 1887.

Kemper, G. W. H., ed. *A Twentieth Century History of Delaware County Indiana,* Chicago: Lewis Publishing Company, 1908.

Kennedy, Joseph. *The Cudahys: an Irish-American Success Story.* Callan, Co. Kilkenny: Michael J. Cudahy, 1995.

Kughn, Linda. Personal interview. June 10, 2000.

"L. A. Young Dies; Noted as Lawyer, Utility Director." Clipping file. Chicago Historical Society.

Leland, Roth M. *Shingle Styles: Innovation and Tradition in American Architecture 1874 to 1982.* New York: Harry Abrams, Inc., 1999.

Leonard, John William, ed. *The Book of Chicagoans.* Chicago: A. N. Marquis & Co., 1905.

Logan, Sheridan. *Old Saint Jo, Gateway to the West, 1799-1932.* 1979.

"Luther Day Dies at 86, Was Lawyer's Lawyer." *The Cleveland Press.* Feb. 8, 1965.

Lydens, Z. Z., ed. *The Story of Grand Rapids.* Grand Rapids, MI: Kregel Publications, 1966.

Manikoff, Jane. Telephone interview. Sept. 2, 2000.

Marquis, Albert Nelson, ed. *The Book of Chicagoans.* Chicago: A. N. Marquis & Co., 1911.

Martin, Trish. Telephone interview. Aug. 14, 2000.

Massie, Larry B. and Peter J. Schmitt. *Kalamazoo, the Place Behind the Product.* Woodland Hills, CA: Windsor Publications, 1981.

Mather, Horace E. *Lineage of Rev. Richard Mather.* Hartford: Press of the Case, Lockwood & Brainard Company, 1890.

Matyn, Chris. Telephone interview. Sept. 18, 2000.

McCabe, John. *Grand Hotel, Mackinac Island.* Detroit: Wayne State University Press, 1987.

Men of Illinois. Chicago: Halliday Witherspoon, 1902.

Michigan Biographies. Lansing: Michigan Historical Commission, 1924.

"Michigan Historic Sites Online." Michigan State Historic Preservation Office. Aug. 16, 2000. <http://www.michsite.state.mi.us>.

Michigan Pioneer and Historical Society Collection, vol. 26. Lansing: The Society, 1888-1912.

Michigan Tradesman, vol. 32. Grand Rapids, MI: Tradesman Co., 1915.

Moran, James B. "Panorama of Old Detroit-Stories of Pedestrians." James B. Moran Page. Oct. 12, 2000 <http://www.merit.edu/~jimmoran/detphot/douglas.html>.

A Most Superior Land, Life in the Upper Peninsula of Michigan. Lansing: Two PeninsulaPress, 1983.

"Mrs. Stockbridge Dead at Mackinac." *Kalamazoo Telegraph,* Aug. 28, 1911.

Musser, Dan and Amelia Musser. Telephone interview. Nov. 17, 2000.

"Obituary Records." Chicago Historical Society, 1886.

"An Old Pioneer Gone." Clipping file. Chicago Historical Society. Sept. 14, 1886.

One Hundred Years of Brewing. Chicago: H.S. Rich & Co., 1903.

The Past and Present: Shiawassee County, Michigan. Lansing: Michigan Historical Publishing Association, 1906.

Peoria Illustrated, 1893. Peoria: Peoria Transcript, 1893.

Peterson, Eugene T. *Mackinac Island, Its History in Pictures.* Lansing: Mackinac Island State Park Commission, 1973.

Petoskey City Directory. 1899.

Porter, Phil. *Mackinac, An Island Famous in These Regions.* Mackinac Island: Mackinac State Historic Parks, 1998.

—. *View from the Veranda.* Mackinac Island: Mackinac State Historic Parks, 1981.

A Portrait and Biographical Record of Delaware County, Indiana. Chicago: A.W. Bowen & Co., 1894.

Portrait and Biographical Record of Kalamazoo, Allegan, and Van Buren Counties, Michigan. Chicago: Chapman Bros., 1892.

"Prominent Islander Passes Away." *Cheboygan Democrat,* Sept. 22, 1921.

Prominent Men of the Great West. Chicago: Manhattan Pub. Co., 1894

Puttkammer, Cordie. E-mail to the author. June 20, 2000.

Puttkammer, Ernst Wilfred. "The Reminiscences of Ernst Wilfred Puttkammer." Interview with Thomas Pfeiffelman. 1973.

"Ramsey County, Minnesota Census." 1860.

Rearick, Carol. E-mail to author. Apr. 8, 2000.

Reed, Monte. *History of the Silverthorne Family.* Privately printed.

—. Telephone interview. Nov. 3, 2000.

Rice, James. *Peoria City and County, Illinois,* vol. 2. Chicago: S. J. Clarke Publishing Company, 1912.

Robertson, Robert S. *History of the Maumee River Basin, Allen County, Indiana,* vol. III. Allen County, IN: Bowen & Slocum, 1905.

"Roland A. Hughes Died at Cygnet." *Daily Sentinel Tribune* [Bowling Green, Ohio], May 25, 1925.

"The Rosicrucian Order." AMORC Home Page. September 6, 2000. <http://www.rosicrucian.org>.

Rutt, Chris L., ed. *History of Buchanan County and the City of St. Joseph.* Chicago: Biographical Publishing Co., 1904.

Roush, Rosalie. Telephone interview. June 2, 2000.

Schmitt, Charlotte. Telephone interview. Apr. 5 and Sept. 8, 2000.

Schueller, Shannon. E-mail to the author. Mar. 24, 2000.

"Services Pending for Law Expert E. W. Puttkammer." *Chicago Tribune.* Mar. 5, 1978.

"Shadows of Life Lengthened Peacefully." *Kalamazoo Daily Telegraph,* July 28, 1900.

Shine, Agnes. "The Reminiscences of Agnes Shine." Interview with Thomas Pfeiffelmann. 1972.

Sicherman, Barbara. *Alice Hamilton: A Life in Letters.* Cambridge, MA: Harvard University Press, 1984.

Silverthorne, M. Landon. E-mail to the author. Nov. 2, 2000.

Sinko, Peggy Tuck. "Dr. Daniel Chemiere Holliday: New Orleans Physician and Early Mackinac Island Cottager." Ms. June 1990.

—. "Hahn Cottage." Ms. July 1972.

—. "Walsh Family." Ms. Jan. 2001.

—. "Warren Family." Ms. Jan. 2001.

St. Ignace Enterprise, July 22, 1915.

Standard Atlas of Peoria City and County, Illinois. Chicago: Geo. A. Ogle & Co., 1896.

"Stephanie Gott, Musician, Dies." *Detroit Free Press,* July 10, 1933.

"Stonecliffe." Ms.

Straus, Frank. "Maple Lodge History." Unpublished ms, July 1, 1984.

Straus, Frank and Brian Leigh Dunnigan. *Walk a Crooked Trail, A Centennial History of Wawashkamo Golf Club.* Mackinac Island: Wawashkamo Golf Club, 2000.

Straus, Lorna. Personal interview. June 15, 2000.

Symon, Charles and Barbara Symon. *U-P People: Some Contributions from the Upper Peninsula of Michigan to the Nation and the World.* Gladstone, MI: RonJonPress, 1987.

Taylor, J. "Mackinac Vistas: A New Spirit for the Grand Hotel Owners' Island Cottage in Michigan." *Architectural Digest,* Vol 47, Aug. 1990, pgs. 166- 171.

Tellefson, Tom. Telephone interview. Sept. 12, 2000.

Timmons, Clayton and Anna Timmons. E-mail to author. Dec. 13, 2000; Dec. 19, 2000; Jan. 5, 2001.

"Tootle's Opera House." *Museum Graphic,* Winter 1963.

Tracy, W. P., ed. *Men Who Make St. Joseph "The City Worth While."* St. Joseph, MO: W. P. Tracy, c.1920.

Valley of the Upper Maumee River, vol. II. Madison , WI: Brant & Fuller, 1889.

The Western Brewer. Apr. 1919.

Williams, Meade C. *Early Mackinac, The Fairy Island.* St. Louis: Bushart Brothers, 1897.

Willoughby, Robert. *Robidoux's Town.* 1997.

Wood, Edwin O. *Historic Mackinac.* New York: MacMillan Co., 1918.

INDEX